Come Fly With Me

Come Fly With Me

'RECOLLECTIONS OF A MARINE FIGHTER PILOT'

Capt Tom Kane USMC

ISBN: 1508971013
ISBN 13: 9781508971016
Library of Congress Control Number: 2015904598
CreateSpace Independent Publishing Platform
North Charleston, South Carolina

Dedication

This book is dedicated to
Judy Kane,
my loving copilot for all of these stories.

Foreword

As the years rolled by, I wanted to write recollections of my five enjoyable years in the Marine Corps. Flying jets was my dream come true.

I have done my best to remember times and places despite the loss of my logbook twenty years ago.

I have strived to put you in the seat with me so that you may feel the exhilaration of my flight experiences—day and night, combat and noncombat flights alike.

I want to alert you, the reader, that two of these chapters are heavy in nature. The episodes have been within me for all these years, and I feel a need to share—lest we forget.

I trust that my fellow squadron mates from VMA-225 will forgive me if I have mixed up their names on certain flights. My memory is very good but short!

I hope you enjoy the ride.

Table of Contents

Introduction

FOR MANY YEARS, I TOYED with the idea of writing some memoirs of our time in the Marine Corps. I didn't want to write a story about me—too over the top and uncomfortable. However, the things that my wife, Judy, and I have done over the past fifty-three years have given rise to so many anecdotes among friends of ours—and in this case, squadron mates—that I felt compelled to attempt something.

In this book of stories, I have tried to put you in my place behind the controls of a fast jet that I was so fortunate to fly. If my syntax suffers, it's from an attempt to give you a first-person feeling behind the controls. Sometimes it works, and other times, the dialogue seems to switch to an instructional tape, all in the desire to convey the true cockpit sensations—the noises, the smells, the visuals, especially at night. Those were my objectives—you will have to judge the results.

IN THE BEGINNING...

I was born in Brooklyn, New York, in 1939, and attended Xavier High School and Fordham University. Having enlisted in the PLC program, I spent the summers of 1959 and 1960 plying the red-clay dust and mud of Quantico, Virginia.

Upon graduation from Fordham in June 1961, I was commissioned a Second Lieutenant and departed for Quantico, Virginia, to begin my active duty with the Marine Corps. In October of that year, I met and fell in love with Judy Molle, a stewardess with United Airlines, based in Washington, DC. After the proverbial whirlwind relationship and my loneliness upon moving on to flight training in Pensacola, we decided to get married in February 1962 and share the venture together. Fifty-three years later, it's still a work in progress— but I cherish every moment of it.

The wedding was an event, as both of our families traveled to Florida for it—Judy's from Iowa and mine from New York. More stories than time to tell them!

TOM AND JUDY KANE
Mustin Beach Officers' Club

I entered preflight training at Naval Air Station Pensacola and then primary training at Saufley Field in the T-34, the only prop-aircraft I ever piloted successfully. (In 1966, I tried my hand at the two-engine Beechcraft, but I never mastered the tail wheel—I was an accident waiting to happen!)

In the late spring of 1962, with my primary training completed, we moved to Meridian, Mississippi, where the twins, Tommy and Teri, were born later that year. We had an instant family of four!

At NAS Meridian, I transitioned to jets—the T2J Buckeye, specifically. My instructor, Captain Jack Rothwell, was later killed in a flying accident in the Philippines. I tried, to no avail, to have his name inscribed on the Vietnam Wall. Judy and I remain friends with his widow, Pat Rothwell, and her sons.

Six months later, there was a brief return to Pensacola for my initial day-carrier qualification in the Buckeye. That challenge completed, we all departed for Iowa and the Christmas break between duty stations.

In January 1963, we headed to Beeville, Texas, for advanced training in the F9F Cougar and the F11F Tiger—both state of the art Grumman aircraft.

T2 BUCKEYE

In the F9, I progressed through my instrument rating and both day and night carrier requalification.

I received my Wings of Gold in March 1963. I had never worked harder—before or since—for anything in my life than I did for my Naval Aviator Wings. I still proudly wear them.

Flight training completed, we were assigned to the Second Marine Air Wing at Cherry Point in North Carolina, and my unit, VMA-225, for the next two and a half of the proudest years of my life. A few months after arriving there, Judy presented us with another girl, Linda, born in the base hospital. Now we were a family of five!

The Cherry Point time was marked by the Cuban Missile Crisis and a deployment to Yuma, Arizona, the month that President Kennedy was assassinated. Vietnam was still an unfamiliar name to all of us.

In September 1964, the squadron deployed for thirteen months to the Far East. Although based in Iwakuni, Japan, we would venture to Okinawa, South Korea, and the Philippines for deployments during the first seven months. Then we redeployed and spent the final five months in Vietnam.

Judy and the children moved to Iowa for the thirteen months. It was nearer to her family. Two months after deployment, Diane was born in Iowa in November of 1964. Now we were a family of six!

In late May 1965, we started moving toward Vietnam via the Philippines—Cubi Point—and landed our first A4s on the mat strip at Chu Lai on June 1, 1965. We operated from Chu Lai until October 1965 when we crossed the Pacific on our way back to Travis, AFB, and effectively disbanded the squadron. I had attained rank of captain and had successfully flown sixty-three combat missions over Vietnam.

At Travis Air Force Base, I remember changing out of my uniform before departing for San Francisco Airport and the civilian flight to Omaha. It had been almost eleven months since I had departed Omaha from emergency leave on December 26, 1964, and thirteen months since the squadron deployed. I felt like I was finally home when I arrived in Iowa.

Our next and final duty station was back to Cherry Point in November 1965. The six of us departed for North Carolina and a surprisingly enjoyable six months before separating from active duty in May 1966—exactly five years since going active.

The first fifteen chapters of this book all occurred during those magical five years, 1961–1966. The sixteenth and final chapter was an unexpected bonus for me forty years later. I will leave it for you to read and, hopefully, enjoy.

EASTER 1967—OUR FIRST HOME, MATAWAN, NJ
TOM, JUDY, DIANE, LINDA, TERI, and TOM JR.

CHAPTER 1

Night Carrier Work

THE EIGHTEEN MONTHS IN THE Training Command are drawing to a (hopefully) successful close. I'm within two months of getting my "Wings of Gold." We've moved to Naval Air Station Beeville, Texas, to fly F9F Cougars and F11F Tigers, both Grumman aircraft. Although I have previously qualified day-carrier landings on the USS *Antietam* back in Pensacola, six months have passed and I have to "requal" in the F9F to stay current. However, the night landings aboard ship are something new.

GRUMMAN F9F COUGAR

The usual "bouncing" (as we referred to practice landings) for both day and night "quals" is scheduled every day. The night practices are now taking on a new meaning and intensity. The adrenaline is really starting to flow!

1

Finally, after a week of intensive practices, the appointed time arrives. In the four months since I had left Pensacola, the USS *Lexington* has replaced the aged USS *Antietam*. Other than that, and the fact that the *"Lex"* has a steam catapult instead of the hydraulic one on the *Antietam,* there are no visible differences between the ships. The all-important feature, the size, is the same—they are both old, small WWII vintage Essex Class carriers.

I get through the day qualifications with the usual tension but no nightmares. Out to the ship, two "touch-and-goes," ten arrested landings, and back to Beeville.

Then come the five night "traps." There are no "touch-and-goes" at night. The night approach pattern is completely different from the day one—there are no visual reference points until the final mile or so.

It's dark when the four-plane division I am in starts up and departs Chase Field, Beeville. The routine is normal—we take off singly and enter an ascending turn, join up on the leader, and head south to the Gulf of Mexico in search of the carrier, sailing about forty miles offshore. We're in loose formation at 28,000 feet, and my nerves are tingling with anticipation. I'm in a cocoon of red instrument lights bouncing off the canopy—it's time to dim the internal lights while watching the wing-lights of the other three planes around me.

As soon as we cross the beach line—"feet wet"—Houston Center instructs us to contact the ship's frequency. Our lead checks in and the *Lexington*'s Approach Control vectors us to a holding point in the sky twenty miles behind the ship. As the ship is moving away at 35 knots, so is the rally point. I listen intently!

Approach Control then instructs each of us to descend to staggered altitudes and enter a holding pattern around that point behind the ship at 21,000 through 25,000 feet altitude. It seems like an eternity but five minutes later we are all in our positions in the holding pattern. As number three, I'm in a racetrack pattern at 23,000 feet.

Then, one plane at a time is released to descend to 20,000 feet and pass through a virtual gate to begin the final descent to the ship. The talk on the radios picks up—I listen closely, afraid to miss my call sign. I'm third in the daisy chain.

The night is pitch-black, and it is like flying in an inkwell. The still invisible ship is sailing away at 35 knots, effectively increasing its relative speed and flattening out the approach pattern. I'm number three in the formation and finally cleared down to and through 20,000 feet—all the way down to 10,000 feet and level. The chatter on the airwaves really increases as all the planes are in descent. Before starting down, I turn the cabin heat to full hot to prevent fogging the cockpit on descent. Although it's minus fifty degrees outside, the cockpit is ninety-plus degrees and, between the heat and tension, I'm completely drenched.

Approaching 10,000 feet, amid all the radio chatter, I hear my call sign—the moment of truth has arrived:

"Chase 12, descend to and maintain 3,000 feet—acknowledge."

I reply, **"Roger—out of 10,000 feet for 3,000 feet."**

There's a natural aversion to reducing power and descending to a lower altitude in total blackness. I scan and rescan all the flight instruments to verify my speed and altitude—every ten seconds! There are no lights aboard a carrier other than the datum lights that simulate a runway and converge to give the illusion of depth and the red flood lights—barely visible even when on deck. It's completely black outside. The dim red glow from the instrument panel provides an eerie reflection off the cockpit glass. There are no other aircraft lights in sight now. I'm alone!

As I approach 3,000 feet, my earphones crackle with the following:

"Chase 12, continue your descent below 3,000 feet. You are on final approach."

I turn down the heat too late; I'm soaked from head to foot. Some of it has been the heat setting but mostly it is nerves.

"Chase 12, call level at 1,000 feet."

I do, and my hand relaxes its death grip on the stick—it has been fighting the need to push forward to descend all the way down. I can feel my heart pounding above the engine whine. I double-check my rate-of-descent indicator to make sure I'm really level and not still descending. I'm level.

A new voice fills my helmet. It's my familiar landing signal officer (LSO) from Beeville, who is aboard the *Lexington.*

"Chase 12, you are five miles from touchdown approaching glide slope."
"Gear and flaps...now."
"Call the ball."

I double-click my mic button to acknowledge.

My left hand leaves the throttle for a second, and I lower the gear and flaps, and back to the throttle. As the gear and flaps descend, my right thumb on the stick makes the subtle trim adjustments.

I'm level at 1,000 feet and a mile and a quarter behind the ship.

Peering ahead I can barely discern the "runway" lights on the ship's deck. Prior to that point, 90 percent of my attention has been inside the cockpit and focused on the instruments with only 10 percent spent scanning outside to see if the ship's lights have become visible. As the deck lights and the "ball" come into focus, the ratios reverse themselves.

When I can clearly see the mirror, I key my mic and say:

"Roger the ball."

The now-familiar voice responds:

> **"Roger the ball—I have you—obey my commands! No further transmissions are necessary."**

Again I double-click on my mic button.

I'm now focused outside the cockpit and only look inside again to confirm my altitude and airspeed as I start down the glide slope toward the ship and touchdown.

Events are moving much faster now!

The final "gate" is six hundred feet and three-fourths mile behind the ship, which is still pulling away from me at 35 knots. From that point until touchdown, the only voice that I hear is the LSO giving me instructions:

> **"You're going low, add power!"**

On the exterior of all Navy aircraft there's a set of lights imbedded in the wing that change from green to amber to red, visually displaying the plane's angle of attack—the angle at which it passes through the air. The LSO watches those lights intensely through binoculars and will be able to detect movements that will affect the aircraft's speed and altitude before the instruments alert the pilot.

> **"Power, power, that's it, hold steady."** My left hand squeezes the throttle forward a bit.

Continuing the descent at night, the phosphorus glow of the ship's wake becomes visible as I cross it and rapidly approach. The net closure rate of 120 knots is really detectable now. Before, all the way down in the darkness, there has been a hazy feeling of being in suspended animation with no sensation of speed, just hanging motionless in the total darkness. If the stars or the moon were out, the ambient light and reflections off the sea would help a bit. Tonight there is no moon.

"Come left two degrees." My right stick hand responds.
"Hold steady, hold steady...you're cleared to land!"

The dark outline of the ship's beam suddenly passes below me, and I slam into the flight deck at the designed four g's. The tail-hook grabs the number 3 wire—I'm a bit long—and I ball up against the instrument panel with the throttle at full power.

The plane has stopped in one hundred fifty feet. There is that unbelievable sense of relief as I uncage my eyeballs and brains and pull the power to idle. The arresting cable is already starting to recoil and is pulling the plane backward as I retract the hook and the cable falls free.

Out of nowhere, a pair of yellow-lighted wands appear in front of my right side giving me the "power-up" signal to clear the landing zone for the next plane careening in behind me. The nose wheel swings around, and I add power and manage to clear the "foul line" just in time.

No time to waste, I'm immediately passed from one set of yellow wands to the next until forty seconds after landing, I'm being positioned on the catapult by a pair of green wands for the next launch. The steam escaping from the catapult shuttle eerily reflects the red and green lights from my wingtips and the rotating beacons on top and below the fuselage.

Following the green wands, I slowly taxi forward onto the catapult shuttle and step on the brakes. The tieback and shear bolt are quickly put in place, and the wands indicate for me to slowly move forward and take up the slack.

Looking out to my right, I can see the catapult officer's rotating wand signaling for me to go to full power, lock the throttle, check my instruments, and hold on.

Pushing the throttle full forward, I turn on the friction lock and wrap my left hand around the throttle and the metal retainer bar to prevent pulling the power off during the eight g acceleration run. I give the engine gauges a quick scan—all is normal—and then flash the wingtip lights as a salute and a signal that all is clear to go. The plane is vibrating wildly at 100 percent power.

The launch officer gives one last visual inspection and listens for anything unusual and then, hearing nothing strange, falls to his knee with the wand pointing forward. In the control room at the side of the deck, the launch button is pressed. My head is back against the ejection-seat headrest as the steam rushes into the catapult. My heart is pounding once again. After what seems an eternity, the combination of engine power and steam pressure reaches the design limit, the shear bolt breaks, and in a millisecond I am on my way. Nothing is going to slow down a catapult launch. If the brakes are on, there are two black stripes down the deck and two flat tires. I am going flying!

There is no way to adequately describe the rush of a "cat shot." Going from a dead standstill to 165 knots in three to four seconds you experience about eight to ten lateral g's of acceleration. Then, at the end of the ramp as the launch shuttle hits the water-break and stops, everything goes dead quiet as the bow of the ship passes silently below. At eighty feet in the air, the acceleration now is solely dependent on the engine as the plane is hurled into the night sky. From landing to launch, the elapsed time has been less than sixty seconds.

As all rookies do, I keep the power at full bore and climb. I'm supposed to level at 600 feet and reenter the left downwind pattern but, as with everyone else, I finally peak around 1,500 feet, turn left, and then fight my natural instincts and finally descend down to the 600-foot level abeam the ship. Now, with the ship's silhouette and phosphorus wake "in view" to my left, and under radar control from the bowels of the ship until I call the "ball" on final, the remaining four landings seem like day traps but without any light.

After the fifth and final landing and launch, the final communication with the ship:

"Chase 12, take a heading of 320; you are 120 miles to home plate. Contact Houston Center. Good night."

An enormous sense of relief and satisfaction sweeps over me, and I really enjoy the ride home. Everyone has departed the pattern and is returning home alone. I check in, and Houston Center clears me to 30,000 feet for the short hop. Twenty minutes later, they clear me below 18,000 feet as I cross the coast and call "feet dry."

"Chase 12, contact Beeville approach. Good night."

The remainder of the flight is routine by now. I shoot a straight-in to Chase Field and into the chocks.

It was two o'clock in the morning when I finally got to our rented quarters. The ever-stalwart Judy and the twins were there, and I am sure they were happy to see me—although Judy never, ever said a word about the risks of my day job.

CHAPTER 2

Flameout

IN 1963, THE BLUE ANGELS had just transitioned from the F9F Cougar to another Grumman airplane, the high performance F11 Tiger. It was the first supersonic aircraft they had flown. That same year the Training Command had the same aircraft at Naval Air Station Beeville, Texas, and I had the privilege of flying them both. This was *Top Gun* stuff long before the movie!

As with the Blues Angels, at Beeville I had just completed my time in the F9F Cougar and was transitioning into the F11 Tiger. This brief time in the supersonic jet was the final hurdle before receiving my Wings.

The flying syllabus for the F11 was centered primarily on tactics and aerial gunnery. It was a fast-moving machine and a beautiful airplane. I still believe it is the most photogenic aircraft the Blue Angels ever flew.

GRUMMAN F11F "TIGER"

Aerodynamically, it's an engine with a pilot stuck in front to guide it and two swept wings to keep it in the air. Functionally, except for the internal thirty-millimeter guns, the airplane serves a very limited tactical mission. However, for several months it is mine to fly, and I certainly enjoy the challenge.

The aerial gunnery range is an area about fifty miles offshore Texas in the Gulf of Mexico, between Houston and Corpus Christie. Typically, the "tractor" or "tow" plane takes off with a cable knot clamped tightly by the speed brake beneath the F11. It's attached to a one-thousand-foot cable that holds a target banner at the far end. To get it airborne, the cable is strewn out on the runway and the F11 executes a short-field takeoff utilizing full afterburner. The steep climb of the F11 lifts the target banner into the air. When airborne with the banner trailing, the "tractor" then heads out to sea and the target range at an altitude of 28,000 feet.

The four student pilots wait until the tractor airplane is halfway to the range. He is dragging the banner at 280 knots, and catching him is not a problem. After the students lift off, they join up in formation and climb to 35,000 feet and 480 knots. By the time the tractor is situated on the range, they have overtaken him.

When we have the tractor in sight below us, the leader takes the formation to the high perch—about one and one-quarter miles to the right and 7,000 feet above the tractor and the banner. Then one after another, we arm our guns and peel off toward the tractor in a rapidly descending left turn to the "low reversal" behind the tractor. It is at this point that the next aircraft peels away and follows the pattern, and so forth until all four aircraft are in the "gun pattern" simultaneously.

At this point, let me explain a few technical terms. The "g" referred to throughout the stories refers to "gravity" and its effect on the pilot. If you are sitting in an airplane on the ground, you are experiencing one "g" or approximately fourteen pounds per square inch of atmospheric pressure. The same would be true if you are in level flight. However, once airborne in a tactical aircraft it is more common that you experience a degree of heightened "g" pressures due to turning and other maneuvers. It is very common to fly the aircraft at pressures up to four g's in combat or tactical formations.

Also, Mach is the speed of sound. The actual airspeed will vary depending on the altitude and the density of the air. At the altitude referred to in this story, it is slightly over 600 knots – a knot being equal to one nautical mile per hour.

Now back to the story.

At the low reversal, we literally snap-roll to the right and start the run on the banner. At this point you're pulling a steady four g's and are going through 30,000 feet at about 600 knots or Mach .96. Here is where the afterburner is engaged to accelerate the plane to supersonic speed, Mach 1.1–1.5, for the actual firing run on the banner. Now you're in a four-g turn at 28,000 feet and supersonic. You're scrunched down into your seat and looking through the top part of your visor with caged eyeballs that are also trying to locate the banner and simultaneously place the gun-sight bullseye on the black ball on the banner. All this while trying to be careful not to shoot the tractor plane instead of the banner!

The first two or three passes are semi-controlled mayhem. All the while you're trying to locate and get the gun-sight on the banner, the plane is coming downhill and accelerating. In a split second you have screamed past the target banner supersonically at Mach 1.15, coming out of "after-burner" and leveling off at 25,000 feet. To take advantage of your speed, you call "off" and then pull back on the stick. You soar over and ahead of the tractor and climb back up the 10,000 feet to the 35,000 feet "perch" for another run. By the time you arrive, the previous plane has just vacated the perch and commenced his run.

After a few runs, you might get an occasional "hit" on the banner—forget a bull's-eye, that would be more of an accident than skill!

Now the stage is set—on to the story!

We have been on the range every morning and afternoon for a week and getting more proficient every day. This is one of the final runs, and I have previously qualified by hitting the banner a few times. I'm sure they were stray shots that happened to find the banner and not the tractor.

We're already on the range offshore Texas.

I roll to the left off the high perch and drop into the slot to accelerate to supersonic speed. After a few seconds, I roll right into the low reversal and come around the detent on the throttle to engage the afterburner—the expected boost in the backside isn't there! Instinctively I look at the airspeed indicator and it's decelerating rapidly. The engine rpms are now below 80 percent and falling—not a good sign!

Leveling my wings, I announce on the radio in as calm a falsetto voice as I can muster:

"FLAMEOUT."

I come back around the idle detent, bringing the throttle into the off position to purge any unburned fuel that may be accumulating in the engine. Then I deploy the RAT, a small, wind-driven emergency turbine generator to maintain electrical power.

By the time I arrive abeam the tractor, which is level at 28,000 feet and 280 knots, I look over and I'm eyeball to eyeball with the pilot. I have slowed down over 300 knots due to the "barn-door" effect of the air in a matter of less than ten seconds.

As I look over, he momentarily opens his speed brakes and the cable and banner head for the Gulf of Mexico, 28,000 feet below.

The tractor pilot, a flight instructor, becomes my wingman and coach as I continue my dead-stick descent. Instinctively, I head for the Texas coastline. Settling into a fast glide, I reach for the emergency book and scan the section titled "Flameout" Reading the notes, I confirm that I have done as prescribed to this point. There is little to do in the next few minutes until I pass below 12,000 feet except pray and think about all the strange fish swimming below me. We're still forty miles offshore, and there is no chance of making landfall. I would run out of air about the time I reached the beach and would be going like a banshee. The choice is limited—either I get the engine restarted or I eject and take my chances with the fish!

Although there seems to be plenty of time to think (and pray) as I glide down to 12,000 feet, it actually is a matter of a few minutes. As long as I keep the nose down and the airspeed adequate, the plane flies as normal. However, I'm descending quickly and we guess that I have two shots at a relight of the engine.

Approaching 12,000 feet, I bring the throttle around the detent and hit the igniters—nothing happens! Although the engine is windmilling at about 40 percent rpm, there is total silence. One shot gone!

I keep descending and fast approaching 10,000 feet—the point of no return. Get the engine lit or punch out!

Then as per the instructions, I reach down to the toggle switch that sits next to the throttle quadrant and pull it up and back to disengage the automatic fuel control function. That function is connected to a barometric unit that reduces fuel flow at higher altitudes where the air is thinner. This prevents the engine from exploding due to more fuel being pumped than oxygen available to burn it. (That's why airplanes burn less fuel at high altitude—thinner air.)

Approaching the 10,000-foot mark, I once again pray and come around the detent, activating the igniters. There's a pause and in a moment, I feel the rumble of the engine relighting and the increasing whine of its compressor accelerating.

My heart restarts as well.

Anxiously I transmit:

"I have a relight."

As the engine stabilizes, I gingerly set the power at 80 percent rpm and head directly for Beeville, Texas, eighty miles away.

While I believe that the problem has been solved, there is an axiom among pilots. When all is well with an airplane, you assume nothing is wrong but when something goes wrong, you assume everything is wrong! I won't relax until I am on the ground!

Ironically, this is the same route I had taken a few weeks before on the way home from night carrier qualifications in the F9F Cougar on the USS *Lexington*. The sense of euphoria is the same but the circumstances are quite different.

I don't dare touch the throttle prior to landing and shoot a straight-in approach to Chase Field. The landing is routine and when I taxi into the chocks, the ground crew climbs all over the airplane. They then order me to flip the toggle switch and return to the automatic fuel mode. I do, and the engine flames out again. The spring that controls the automatic unit is designed to shut the engine down if it fails. It has worked as designed.

From that point until I stopped flying, that was the only incident of major equipment failure that I ever experienced in Navy or Marine aircraft, save for the usual radio nightmares. The design and maintenance of our military aircraft prevent these planes from breaking. Unfortunately, the pilots do break from time to time.

Two weeks later, on the May 28, 1963, in the presence of Judy and the twins, I receive my Navy Wings of Gold and designation as a naval aviator. I had never worked harder for anything in my life, and I still proudly wear my lapel wings today.

ANECDOTE:

While these practice missions were fun and exciting, they instilled a skill and discipline that was put to good use in Vietnam a few years later. Out of Chu Lai in August of 1965, we were providing air cover all night for a Marine unit under attack during "Operation Starlight." They were pinned down in the foothills west of us, and there was no chance of evacuation until dawn. Flying A4s at that time, and operating under the flickering light from parachute flares dropped from 10,000 feet, four of us at a time, hour after hour, executed the very same pattern, albeit slower, that we learned in the F11 gunnery school. The firing altitude was just above treetop and the high perch was at 1,500 feet. The flight pattern was identical and the station calls the same—this time in illuminated darkness and much lower altitude. On several occasions, the parachute flares would extinguish and in total darkness, the position calls kept the planes in order. From 420 knots and 500 feet, there were no misses. Bull's-eyes with our twenty-millimeter guns and rockets were certainly not accidents.

The old saying that "practice makes perfect" has some real meaning when you least expect it. For a Marine aviator, that night in Vietnam was the greatest possible satisfaction—protecting our Marines on the ground no matter the danger or challenge.

CHAPTER 3

Yuma—1963

THE NOW MUCH-ANTICIPATED DEPLOYMENT TO Yuma commenced in mid-November 1963. The squadron was split in two: one division refueling at NAS Memphis and the other at NAS Olathe, Kansas. We then rejoin up at Kirtland AFB, in Albuquerque, New Mexico. This was the farthest west I had ever traveled. We're to spend the night at Kirtland and then, starting at 8:00 the next morning, launch individually and fly a "burner route" to Yuma. A burner route is a low-level flight at one hundred feet above ground and 420 knots. There are no navigation aids en route, and the flights are planned as DR (dead reckoning) navigation exercises. There was obviously no satellite navigation assistance at the time. Every pilot has prepared low-level sectional maps in connected strips with the proper headings and time tics boldly displayed on the knee maps. At one hundred feet and seven miles a minute, there is very little time to go looking for directions.

We land about 4:00 p.m. and, after checking into the Bachelor Officer's Quarters, head for the officers' club and the bar. The group of us sitting there notices the staff wheeling additional portable bars into the club. When I inquire, the bartender points to the TV screen and tells us that the Air Force Academy and New Mexico are playing football downtown and when the game was over, we could probably sell our seats at the bar. An hour later his prediction proved correct.

If we thought that the Mustin Beach "O" Club had great happy hours, Kirtland O Club was to a different power. The food and drinks flowed virtually all night and we, as Marines, enjoyed a degree of pre-eminence among the patrons.

Having used up all of our social ammunition by 5:00 a.m., we finally surrender and head back to the BOQ for a shower, shave, and then gallons of coffee and breakfast in the flight mess. Hung over is not the word—we haven't progressed to that stage yet.

I've scheduled my launch in the first batch, simply because I was the scheduling officer, and back in Cherry Point, I thought it made sense. At 0700, I am seriously questioning my judgment as well as my flying skills. However, throwing all caution to the wind, I launch on time, 0810, right behind the skipper, Colonel Baker.

Recovering from a hangover is amazing when you are on 100 percent oxygen. By the time I lift off, all my faculties are up and running. While I may have cheated a bit on the 100-foot altitude as there was no way to check me, I maintain the proper speed to make the checkpoints and arrive at Yuma on time and in one piece. It is quite an accomplishment!

The only incident we had was when approaching Yuma, one of our pilots, in his A4, managed to land immediately behind a prop-cargo plane and put fourteen g's on the aircraft, condemning it to a major overhaul operation. Fortunately, that was the only casualty of the journey.

The desert flying in Yuma is pure enjoyment. We practice the several delivery methods for a nuclear weapon that, allegedly, gives the pilot at least an even-money chance of getting away from the blast. Fortunately, no one to date has had to test that theory.

All the bomb delivery tactics for "special" weapons (nuclear bombs) involve low-level flying. This is to avoid radar detection on the run-in to the target. The tricky part involves getting the non-afterburner A4 Skyhawk to the proper speed for several of the maneuvers—500 knots.

The only way to get the Skyhawk to 500 knots at sea level is to start accelerating while still coming downhill. For all the approaches, the altitude is 100 feet above the ground! So the object of this exercise is to accelerate to 500 knots several miles before the target and run-in at 100-feet altitude. This is very demanding flying—you have to pay close attention outside the aircraft at that height and speed—880 feet per second.

A year later while on a similar practice run in Korea, one of our squadron mates, First Lieutenant (1/Lt) John Floyd, hit the water on the range just south of Osan. The tide was ebbing and like a mirror. He apparently lost track of his altitude as he was accelerating and it was over in a second. The largest piece of the plane that was recovered was the engine compressor, about the size of a mailbox.

It's about 10:20 on Friday, November 22, and a number of the other pilots are hanging around my desk as I work on Saturday's flying schedule. We've been in Yuma a week. Suddenly on the ready room radio, we hear the terrible announcement that President Kennedy has been shot in Dallas. The news is electrifying. As a combat squadron, we are put on "alert" status until the situation is clarified. All flying ceases.

By Monday the situation has been contained, and we resume our training schedule, albeit with the pall of the assassination and the funeral dominating the discussions. We have three weeks to go, and the damper on the deployment remains with us until we get home.

The voyage home is a story unto itself! We have strong winter winds and can make the trip with only one refueling stop. Half the squadron heads for NAS Memphis, and my group is routed back through Olathe, Kansas. While en route, we receive word that Cherry Point has been shut down due to a severe storm heading up the East Coast.

I'm flying wing on the executive officer, Major Don Gillum. Don came to us from test-pilot school at NAS Patuxent River and is the best pilot in the squadron. He is a great "stick man" and everyone enjoys flying with him. He is also a wild man when it comes to socializing, so again, everyone enjoys being with him.

Major Gillum and I land in Olathe, Kansas with the temperature hovering around zero. Through a bit of luck and rank pulling, he manages to get our two planes into a hangar for warmth. None of the other ten pilots are quite that lucky. It's good to fly with the "Boss."

The departure party that we enjoyed the night before in Yuma recommences again, this time in the Olathe BOQ. My last recollection was a group of us carrying the jukebox up a flight of stairs for some ungodly reason.

The next morning we receive an "all clear" to proceed to Cherry Point.

The race is on!

Major Gillum wants to beat the skipper, Colonel Baker, back to home plate. Our good fortune is still running as he and I have the only planes that don't have a "wet start" due to the extremely low temperatures. Off we go to Cherry Point!

With substantial tailwinds due to the weather, we cover the distance to Raleigh-Durham in about two hours. Normally, at RDU, flight control commences a gradual descent for the final approach to Cherry Point, 150 miles away. It's a rational way to do things.

Don Gillum has another concept!

As we descend through 18,000 feet and exit high-level control, Major Gillum cancels our IFR flight plan, and I'm now in for the ride of my life. Instead of reducing power, he gives the head nod to go full power. I comply, and my heart starts to race like a trip-hammer. At 480 knots going downhill, we cover the remaining distance in about fifteen minutes. The weather is crystal clear and the wind is crisp and out of the northwest, so we have to make a left-hand sweeping turn over Newport and toward Morehead City. Don "calls the runway in sight" ten miles to our left, and I'm holding on for dear life. I'm ten feet away from his plane and suddenly we are in a sixty-degree left turn at 1000 feet over the scratch pines of North Carolina. We're pulling four g's and all I can see are the rivets on the bottom of his plane and his wingtip for separation. The trees and ground flash by under my left wing as if I can touch them.

Unbeknownst to Don, since he cannot see me—I am below him in the turn—I manage to get myself into a "JC" (Jesus Christ) maneuver. With all the stress on the plane and my death grip on the stick, I start to vacillate up and down a few feet at a clip. The reason it's called a "JC maneuver" is because that is what you're shouting into your mask—the speed and the turn angle has caused me to over-correct the movements of the stick. Even though the movements are relatively small, they are exaggerated by the speed. I have gotten behind the aircraft. By the time I should be releasing pressure, however slight, on the stick, it is too late and I should actually be tightening the grip. The normal solution for this phenomenon is to release the stick completely and the aircraft will dampen out the movements by itself. The problem now is I am holding a steady four g's in a steep left turn and barely above the treetops. I'm not releasing any stick!

After what seems an eternity, Don has us lined up with the runway and rolls out level—we slowed a bit in the turn but are still doing 420 knots! I recover completely and sit ten feet off his right wingtip. We arrive over the "numbers" at the end of the runway in a few seconds and he breaks left for landing. I count to three and do the same thing. However, our speed is such that I cannot slow down enough to extend the speed brakes to help slow the plane down. The momentum of speed and the three seconds have taken me halfway to New Bern—and now I must come back to Cherry Point.

Finally in the downwind leg at 250 knots, I put out the speed brakes. By this time I've started my turn into final approach and still going too fast for the gear and flaps. I slip and slide the aircraft to kill speed and at the last minute manage to get the gear and flaps down just prior to touchdown. By the time we taxi in, my heart rate is almost back to normal and, except for the sweat stains down to my ankles, all is well. Another day at the office!

Judy is there for me with the children, and we have a wonderful family photo of our triumphant return from Yuma!

CHAPTER 4

A Night Flight

I LOVE FLYING AT NIGHT—SITTING in the cockpit with the red glow from the instrument lights bouncing off the canopy, the darkness of it all outside. It's always mesmerizing to me.

Let me tell you about my most memorable noncombat flight at night.

It is the summer of 1964, when I need some night flight time to remain current. I file the flight plan of my dreams. It is a simple one. After sunset, I will leave Cherry Point, NC, and fly to New York City and back. I have flown the route several times and landed at Floyd Bennett Field for visits back home in Brooklyn. However, this time my plan is a bit different in that I will not be stopping and landing when I got to New York. I will simply remain at altitude, turn around, and fly back to Cherry Point, NC.

I need about three hours of nighttime to remain current—aviation regulations. It's dusk when I go to the flight line and check out my A4 Skyhawk for the evening.

After the routine preflight inspection, I climb the ladder and get strapped into the seat. The auxiliary power unit (APU) is already whining away—splitting the otherwise quiet evening air. The evening is cool and the sky is clear from North Carolina to New York.

I give the signal to start the engine and the familiar loud whoosh of air from the APU flows into the engine. After a few seconds, as the compressor turns through 5 percent rpm, I bring the throttle around the off-detent and the igniters started clicking away. In a moment, ignition takes place and the dull roar of the jet engine replaces the whine of the APU. At 45 percent rpm, I signal to disconnect the air and the engine settles at 60 percent idle. The power and electrical umbilical cords are disconnected. The A4 is on its own power now.

Reaching back on my right, I push in all the radio and navigation circuit breakers. The needles start to swing in circles, and the gyros start their caging dance. The red interior and instrument lights are on full bright while I sit in the chocks. It is not totally dark, and there is considerable stray light coming from the hangar area.

The radio crackles in my earphones. I'm on ground control to receive flight clearance and can listen to other transmissions, so I know it is working. My eyes scan all the engine indicators—they are normal. A pilot is constantly scanning his instruments looking for the abnormal—the normal doesn't draw attention, it's the one out of sequence that jumps out at you.

I fasten my oxygen mask and close the canopy to shut out the noise of the engine. The cool oxygen always feels good. Ready to go, I key the radio and check in with ground control.

"Charlie Echo 14, ready for clearance."

There is a moment of silence and then the tower comes alive:

"Charlie Echo 14, are you ready to copy?"

I give an affirmative and then begin to copy the flight plan that I had filed a half-hour before. It has been cleared through Norfolk, Washington, and New York Traffic Control Centers during the interim. My route will take me over Norfolk and the Chesapeake Bay area, just east of Washington, DC, and on to New York City, directly overhead Idlewild Airport. Then, after a 180-degree turn, I'll return along the coastline.

With my clearance now in hand, I signal for the chocks to be pulled and, once clear, taxi toward the runway. Cleared onto the northwest runway, I head for the middle apron in front of the tower.

Moving into takeoff position, I press the microphone key and indicate:

"Charlie Echo 14, ready to go."

I am instructed to contact departure control on another frequency. Changing channels, I make contact with departure control—they clear me for immediate takeoff.

I sweep the cockpit with the stick to make sure all the control surfaces are clear and double check the flaps at 50 percent. Pushing the throttle forward, slowly at first, then straight to 100 percent rpm, I'm on my way!

With just fuel on board, the A4 accelerates very quickly. By the time I have rolled twenty-five hundred feet, the plane is ready to fly. I pull back gently on the stick and in a few seconds it is airborne. With a flick of my left hand, the gear and flaps retract. By the time I pass over the end of the runway, the A4 is at 240 knots and accelerating rapidly.

Climbing out, I turn right to head north and at 1,500 feet. I'm directed by departure control to contact Norfolk Center on their frequency, followed by:

"CE 14, have a good evening."

I change frequency and announce to Norfolk Center:

"Charlie Echo 14 airborne, out of 2,500 feet, climbing to flight level two-zero." (20,000 feet)

Norfolk Center responds immediately and requests an "ident"—that means activating the plane's transponder, which emits a discreet radar signal that identifies my aircraft to them. In a moment, they confirm my transponder on their radar screen and clear me from FL-20 (20,000 feet) all the way to FL-36 (36,000 feet) en route. They have already slotted me into the busy northeast traffic corridor.

The twinkling farm lights of North Carolina give way to the increasingly congested tidewater area of Norfolk. In ten minutes, I'm passing through 30,000 feet and climbing. Ahead of me, Norfolk spreads forever. The lights in the distance seem to go from horizon to horizon, broken only by the waterways flowing into the Chesapeake. I've been airborne for twenty minutes and Langley Air Force Base is beneath me. Now level at 36,000 feet, I have engaged the autopilot so I can look around and enjoy the flight. There is no moon and the starlight throws shadows on my lap. I turn down the red instrument lights to reduce the glare off the canopy.

Off to the right I spot the intermittent string of lights that are part of the Chesapeake Bay Tunnel. It was only six months ago that I was in survival training with the Coast Guard at Langley. How well I remember being dropped into the bay with only my one-man raft on which to survive. I was in the water at 0800 and by 1600 had drifted almost to the Bay Tunnel. For the last two hours I was convinced that they had forgotten about me. Just prior to mashing my personal panic button, the rescue boat came over the horizon—a welcome sight. Now, from this height, I had a different perspective and appreciation for the size and scope of Chesapeake Bay.

With Baltimore my next checkpoint, I continue flying up the bay and can see the lights of Washington, DC, at 11:00 p.m. in the distance. Flying abeam Quantico in the darkness, I remember it was only a few years since Judy and I had met there. Time and events have gone by quickly. Our third child, Linda, has recently been born at Cherry Point Hospital.

To the east, across the Delmarva Peninsula, I can see out to the ocean. There is no horizon, only a guess where the starlit sky disappears into the black sea. With a new moon tonight, it is very, very dark. But for the passing lights below, there's no sensation of speed at night. It's like suspended animation. I love it.

Quickly I'm upon DC. The bright lights of the monuments shine upward. The clear pattern of the street design becomes obvious at this altitude. On the ground it's another story. The ovals surrounding the White House and the Washington Monument are easy to discern by the darkness of the grounds around them. I think it's ironic that the lack of light in this sea of light makes it easier to find things.

Washington has slipped by my left side, and Baltimore and Wilmington are dead ahead. Looking up, the starlight envelops the cockpit. It reminds me of sitting in a planetarium. The difference is that the stars are fixed and I'm moving at seven miles per minute. There's a surreal feeling to night flying. All you have are the sounds of the airplane and the radio blurbs from time to time. I'm in rapture.

I report overhead Baltimore and shortly receive instructions to contact New York Center on a different frequency along with another:

"Charlie Echo 14, have a nice evening," from below.

I wonder if they are aware that I'll be returning to their control within the hour—I'm sure they are.

Baltimore and Wilmington silently slide behind. Now the lights of Philadelphia are off to my left. In front of me is the vast Delaware River basin, outlined by the darkness of it. I can detect the small town of Cape May on the New Jersey side of the river. Then the lights are very scattered ahead—all the farms and small towns of rural New Jersey. Off to the east, on the coast, I can see the lights of Atlantic City. Not much there this time of year. Gambling and the nightlife are still years away.

Halfway up the Jersey coast, the lights of the New York metropolitan area start to fill the front canopy. Although way below me, they seem to stretch as far as I can see. The coastline is a study in geography. Long Island stretches to the northeast horizon outlined by the darkness of the ocean and Long Island Sound. The Hudson River slices through the sea of lights between New York and New Jersey. Manhattan and Staten Island are easily discernible.

I've never seen New York City from this height before. All the lights appear white from this altitude—an interesting phenomenon.

I'm rapidly approaching my "destination"—Idlewild Airport. As the navigation instruments spin slowly to indicate station passage, my next checkpoint, Salisbury, Maryland, is behind me. I commence a 180-degree turn to my left, to keep the city in view, and report in to New York Center and confirm my altitude. The perfunctory acknowledgment is given. There is no comment regarding the nature of my flight plan. I wonder how many other pilots do this.

In the thirty-degree bank turn, I'm able to look down and pick out many familiar sights in Brooklyn. Greenwood Cemetery and Prospect Park easily standout—again, the absence of lights! It's difficult to pick out a particular street, but I can discern the main thoroughfares. There is Flatbush and Church Avenue—the Dutch Church graveyard is dark. It helps pinpoint it.

My eyes travel to the Parade Grounds near Prospect Park, another black spot. This is my old neighborhood—what a thrill!

I think of my parents down there now. Would they be proud to know I was up here watching them? I'll call tomorrow to tell them I was up for a visit!

I glance over to the Lower Manhattan area—the tall buildings are barely distinguishable from above. But again, Trinity graveyard stands out in its blackness. That leads me to the corner of Wall Street and Broad Street. The World Trade Centers are still ten years away! All that is there now is the blackness of the Hudson River.

Directly below me is a necklace of lights across the Narrows between Brooklyn and Staten Island. These are the main suspension cables for the still-unfinished Verrazano Bridge. I wonder to myself what will happen to the ferries.

I pick out the docks in Staten Island where in 1946 we all waited for my cousin Don to disembark from the troopship bringing him home from WWII. More than a bit of nostalgia comes over me. How privileged I am to be up here and overlooking my heritage. Suddenly, I get a bit of a chill. It's cold outside, so I turn up the heat.

Completing my turn, I have to level the wings, and the lights and sights of New York City below me fall away. No time for a second turn, I've been cleared to Salisbury via Atlantic City.

The journey back home goes quickly; it always seems that way. Passing over Atlantic City, I switch from New York Center back to Baltimore Center. A familiar voice rings in my ear.

"Charlie Echo 14, ident."

I do, and a few seconds later he confirms my status and the radio goes silent again. The airwaves have gotten quiet at this time of night. Not much other traffic at this altitude in 1964.

The engine is purring and the miles are clicking away at seven a minute. I'm following the coastline back to Cherry Point—a more direct route than the one northward. The blackness of the ocean is on my left now and a few farm lights of rural Maryland flicker below me all the way to the small town of Salisbury.

Shortly thereafter, I am instructed to contact Norfolk Center followed by the now familiar:

"CE 14, have a good evening."

I thank Baltimore Center for their assistance and switch channels.

In another ten minutes I'm once again over the Bay Tunnel, cutting across the blackness of Chesapeake Bay and approaching Virginia Beach.

Twenty minutes past the Norfolk area, I'm instructed to commence my descent into Cherry Point. Heat up full, power back to 60 percent, and nose down. I'll maintain my 420 knots until reaching the twenty-five-mile airport zone or instructed to slow down for some traffic reason. I'm about 110 miles out. In less than twenty minutes, I should be on final approach.

As I leave positive radar control descending through 18,000 feet, Norfolk Center tells me to contact Cherry Point Approach Control. Another "good evening" and I continue my descent. By the time I connect with Cherry Point, I report passing 15,000 and they clear me to 10,000 feet. In reply I am requested to once again "ident." I comply and hear my instructions:

"Charlie Echo 14, we have you on radar—continue your descent to 3,000 feet."

Passing 10,000 feet, I turn the red cabin lights up a bit and the heat down a bit. I need to see the instruments better and the cabin-fogging problem is behind me now. All is well. Now I need to pay attention to my flight indicators more than my navigation gear. I know where I am and so does Approach Control. They will steer me home from here. I need to make sure that I maintain proper altitude, attitude, and airspeed. Priorities change when you get closer to the ground. That's where the accidents happen.

At thirty-five miles out, starting to level 3,000 feet, I have to add power and reduce airspeed at the same time. At 80 percent rpm my speed will slow to 250 knots—the maximum speed for any aircraft within twenty-five miles of an airport. It's an easy transition. By the time I get to twenty-five miles on my DME, I have settled at 250 knots and leveled at 3,000 feet. At this altitude, the ground lights create a sensation of speed that was absent at higher levels.

The weather is still clear and the same runway is in use. Approach Control vectors me toward Morehead City and a right-hand turn onto final approach. Although taking my directions from Approach Control, I'm able to see the runway from a distance and report it in sight. "Roger" comes back. At five miles I'm told to commence my descent. I pull the power back and push the nose forward a bit to start down. At 1,500 feet and a mile and a half, speed brakes out, gear and flaps down, I begin slowing down to 140 knots prior to landing. All the while listening, I look for the "ball," the visual landing aid that will guide me to touchdown. As soon as I can see it, I call "the ball" and Approach Control acknowledges and releases me for a visual landing. I'm instructed to contact the tower on ground control after landing.

A minute later, I'm rolling out and exiting the runway. Contacting ground control, they clear me to the VMA-225 parking area. Another few minutes of taxi, and I'm being guided into the chocks by a set of illuminated wands. The chocks are inserted under the wheels and after a brief check, I get the cutoff signal from the plane captain. I'm home, and one of my most enjoyable flights has come to an end. Fifty years later, I remember it as if it was yesterday.

The next day I phone both my father and mother to tell them I was looking down on them last evening.

CHAPTER 5

A Visit To K. I. Sawyer AFB

THERE IS A LULL IN the official flight training schedule, so two of us, Lieutenant Harry "Slick" Slacum and I decide to take the opportunity to do cross-country flying under the guise of further training. The sorties do provide an opportunity to get more flight time. Harry and I will decide where to go. We will take a stack of fuel chits and head off for the day. That morning, in the late spring of 1964, the weather at Marine Corps Air Station Cherry Point is clear. Our squadron, VMA-225, has a party scheduled for the weekend so someone is needed to fly to Naval Air Station Brunswick—for lobsters! This is a good excuse for a nice flight to Maine. Each plane has an old three-hundred-gallon fuel tank on the center station, customized for carrying baggage as well as two fuel tanks on each wing station.

The elapsed flight time to Brunswick is only two hours each way—not very interesting. So Slick and I decide we need an intermediate stop. We want to find somewhere we have never been before.

In the old days, every squadron had a large map on a wall with a string tacked to the home station and it could be stretched in any direction. Facing the map, Harry and I discuss possible destinations. We finally decide on K. I. Sawyer Air Force Base in Marquette, Michigan. We'll refuel there and head east to Brunswick, Maine, for the lobsters and then back home to Cherry Point.

Before weather satellites, a visit to the weather gurus who practiced the science (mostly art) of predicting and reporting weather was a necessity. The weather maps were a product of visual observations, balloon releases, and isobar readings from weather stations across the country. Aside from the guesswork involved, there was also a built-in delay of several hours between readings. We give the weather map a cursory study, note a cold front moving into the upper-Midwest, and head for our two A4 Skyhawk jets.

The flight line is always alive with activity at this time of the morning. The air is punctuated with the low cadence of engines starting and belching exhaust flames as their engines ignite. The smell of JP-4 fuel starts my adrenaline going—that unique pungent odor that I love so much. It was memorialized years later by Robert Duval in *Apocalypse Now*. Napalm is simply jet fuel with a sticking agent powder mixed into it. When burning, they smell the same!

A quick but thorough preflight and check of the baggage tanks complete, I climb the ladder to the cockpit and slide onto my ejection seat. With a little help strapping in from my plane captain, Angelo Lemme, I'm ready to start the engine. Harry is doing the same three planes further down the flight line. As the auxiliary power unit roars to life, I give the twirling finger signal to open the intake valve and start feeding the compressed air into the engine. With a sharp eye on the rpm indicator, my left hand is wrapped around the throttle. When the engine rpm reaches 5 percent, I move it forward and around the shut-off detent—the same as taking a car out of park—and wait for the low thump as the engine ignites behind me. The low, throaty rumble gathers pitch and vibrates slightly as the rpm indicator slowly accelerates. When it gets to 45 percent, I give Angelo the plug-out signal, and the external power is chopped and the air hose disengaged. The powerful jet engine continues to accelerate on its own. About twenty seconds into the process, the engine has settled at 60 percent idle rpm. The exhaust temperature has peaked and already fallen back to normal as the airflow increases. I flick on all the switches and push in the circuit breakers for the electronics. Needles jump to life. The gyros dance on their gimbals. After a quick scan of all the instruments, I flash a thumbs-up to Lemme. The external electrical umbilical is disconnected. The plane and I are on our own now with the engine whining and instruments flickering. Slick, my wingman, has done the same, and we signal each other that we are ready to go.

It's time to leave all the familiar smells and sounds of the line behind us, so I fasten my mask firmly, lower the canopy, and start to suck in the 100 percent oxygen from the onboard liquid oxygen tank. I trigger the microphone for ground control and receive confirmation of our flight plan to Michigan and our taxi instructions. As custom, when cleared to taxi, the external wing lights are lit, and I salute my plane captain before exiting the chocks. The tower has cleared us to the takeoff position.

Adding power, I leave the chocks. Slick follows me, and we bounce along the taxiway in tandem. As the senior pilot, I am in command of the flight. Six minutes later we are in position and cleared for takeoff.

Harry and I take off in formation to save time and fuel. Both planes are side by side on the runway—he slightly right and aft of me. I give the power-up signal—twirling index finger—and we push the throttles forward simultaneously, slowly at first and then straight to 100 percent rpm. The planes accelerate quickly. Even with a full fuel load, we reach our takeoff speed of 160 knots in 2,500 feet, rotate the noses together, lift off, and immediately retract the gear and flaps. Ten seconds later the gear doors slam shut beneath me, and we cross the end of the runway at 240 knots. We accelerate rapidly to 360 knots, our ideal climbing speed. Leaving Cherry Point behind, we head northwest. Twenty minutes later, we have settled in for K. I. Sawyer AFB at 36,000 feet and our cruising speed of 420 knots.

As we climb out, Slick slides out to "high station," about a quarter mile off my right wing and up about one hundred feet. This allows him to observe me and any unannounced traffic coming our way.

The first hour is a series of routine handoffs from one control center to the next. It becomes second nature to pick up your own callsign amid all the chatter on the airwaves.

The first sign that we might have a problem is on the handoff to Indianapolis Center when my transmitter becomes intermittent. I don't think much of it at the time. Radio problems are fairly common in these days of radio tubes, but it is an omen of things to come!

The second indication that troubles lay ahead is when we come upon a thick cirrus cloud layer at 36,000 feet. The density of the cloud cover at this altitude is also ominous. The cold front is fast approaching—and we are heading straight into it. Within fifteen minutes, Slick has moved to within one hundred feet of my wing position so we can maintain visual contact. I assume that the clouds are layered beneath us. This is an error in judgment—they are solid to the ground.

Approaching northern Indiana, my transmitter doesn't get any better. I can hear everything, but I am unable to transmit. As we come upon Chicago, Slick announces that his navigation equipment is failing and he really does not know where we are or where we are going. This compounds our problem. I know I have to keep the lead despite my radio transmission problems.

Switching frequencies, I can hear the ground instructions. I scramble to write down the frequency numbers, and Harry acknowledges the transmissions for both of us. Meanwhile, I concentrate on the navigation part of the flight. We leave Chicago behind us and are approaching Green Bay when we are handed over to Minneapolis Control. No apparent problem as we use hand signals to confirm the station frequencies. Outside, the weather is getting very ugly.

As we come up on the Minneapolis frequency, they tell us there is some traffic ahead, and we will have to enter a holding pattern. This is not good news. Holding in a racetrack pattern, ten-mile legs and 180-degree turns for twenty minutes is problematic. We will be burning fuel and essentially standing still over the ground.

Cruising at 420 knots is seven miles per minute—a twenty-minute hold costs us 140 miles of progress! To make our fuel situation worse, traffic control then orders us to descend in the holding pattern to 20,000 feet, thus burning more fuel at the lower altitude. I nod and

Slick acknowledges the transmission. I signal to reduce power, and we start to descend.

While it is hard work for me, this is a nightmare unfolding for Harry. I look through my sweat-filled visor over at him—he is about twenty feet away and his eyes are glued to my helmet as a reference point. Although every plane is slightly different, there is an imaginary line that extends from the lead pilot's helmet past the front wing-light and into infinity. The other planes in formation align themselves along that invisible line and slide in and out depending on visibility. Today there is no visibility; Slick is twenty feet away and hanging really tight.

Harry calls ground control for a weather check. They are still calling the weather at K. I. Sawyer as 1,500 feet and one-mile visibility. Again, no apparent problem but in my gut, I just don't believe them. Experience has taught me that things are turning to shit really fast!

As if it wasn't warm enough, before descent I had turned the temperature to "full-hot" to prevent fog from developing inside the cockpit and obscuring the canopy. I hardly notice the ninety-degree-plus heat at this point.

The cirrus clouds have morphed into ink-black storm clouds and the occasional lightning flashes keep my attention. I'm sweating profusely by now—sweat soaks my flight suit down to my ankles. My gloves are wet and sticking to everything. Thank God for the oxygen—it keeps me from hyperventilating. We descend in the racetrack pattern as ordered, and by the third time around the loop in the now-dense cloud cover, Slick can't tell which side is up. My eyes are like saucers. I'm relying totally on the instruments to keep us in the air. Slick is relying on me!

At 20,000 feet traffic control straightens us out and finally vectors us toward K. I. Sawyer. Again driving rain pelts the canopy! A very bad feeling has come over me so I look for any alternative field to land. The only possibility was Kinchelow AFB off to the east but it is now out of range. There are no alternatives—we are going to Marquette, Michigan, come hell or high water!

As we turn onto the "final approach" into K. I. Sawyer, I notice that we still have seventy miles yet to go. I think this has to be an Air Force base with an approach like this. Another gulp and more sweat! Now fuel is a critical concern. For the moment we are okay, but there is no slack if we have trouble getting these planes on the ground. Minneapolis Center clears us for further descent—the usual hand-signal gymnastics, and Slick checks us in. We're getting lower and, even with reduced power, we're burning more of our precious fuel.

Twenty-five miles from the runway and we are finally given the frequency change to K. I. Sawyer Approach Control. I listen to the frequency, write it down, confirm the numbers by hand signals with Slick, and dial in the radio channel. Slick announces our arrival and there is a deadly silence. My heart stands still! I hold my breath. No comeback—total silence! Then, after two more broadcasts and what seems an eternity, a voice finally comes back to us. My heart starts again. Thank God, it is ground control. I can only guess the delay is because the control staff can't believe that anyone was actually going to attempt to land airplanes there today.

Our jets do not have the newest instrument landing system (ILS) on board.

We are now under the radar control of Sawyer Approach for a ground-controlled approach (GCA) landing. That means that the radar operator will have to direct us to a point in the sky where we will intercept two imaginary lines. One line is an extension of the runway and the other is an ascending line starting at the runway and rising to infinity on a sloping angle, creating a glide-slope. I pray that the controller is on his game today!

Time and fuel are moving quickly now. We have slowed to 250 knots—four miles per minute—but at the lower altitude it always seems much faster. The rain and clouds are pelting the canopy. The controller guides us to intersect those two lines at 4,000 feet, and we immediately reduce power and commence our final descent. Slick reports us out of 4,000 feet and on the way down.

Control is still calling airport weather at 1,500 feet and one-mile visibility. The runway altitude is 1,225 feet above sea level, so we have about 2,500 feet of air beneath us—assuming there are no hills between us and the runway. I settle us in for a final approach, squinting through the single windowpane with the small windshield wiper flailing away.

There is still no letup in the blinding rain. Slick is in position about ten feet off my right wing and holding on for dear life. His fate, for better or worse, is totally dependent upon me. That's the way it is in military aviation.

The radar controller crackles instructions through the silence into my earphones and I nod to Slick, who acknowledges transmissions with double-clicks on his microphone button. No time to speak.

We press forward into the rain. Despite the unbelievable tension, it feels surreal. It is as if we are in suspended animation. The controller calls the five-mile marker and we drop our gear, flaps, and speed brakes, and report passing down through 3,000 feet. Now we have slowed to 140 knots for landing. We are 1,700 feet above the ground.

My eyeballs are caged to the instrument panel with intermittent glances out of the canopy to see if the ground has become visible yet. The heat is still at full hot and the sweat is pouring down my face and into my mask. There is nothing but driving rain—the A4 has a small windshield wiper like a car and it's in overdrive on the front windscreen panel ahead of the gun-sight.

We continue to descend. At 2,500 feet I should see glimpses of ground below us but nothing is visible. We go to "minimums" at 1,800 feet—still nothing! The radar controller keeps confirming that we were on centerline and glide-slope, but at 1,500 feet (300 feet above the ground) we are told we are below landing minimums and to "ABORT THE LANDING"! That means climb out and go around for another approach!

I have already determined that although our fuel state will probably allow one more approach, and then what? I hear the transmission but decide that this approach is as good as it is going to get. We continue to descend in the fog and driving rain. Slick obviously agrees as he doesn't acknowledge the instructions with the usual double-click on the mic button.

Suddenly, at fifty feet above the ground, the green datum lights for the runway threshold pass beneath my aircraft and we immediately hit the runway. Because Slick is below me, he strikes the runway first and it scares the shit out of him! I follow a millisecond later even though I was ahead of him. Knowing that all Air Force bases have long runways, we decide to avoid the brakes and let the planes slow down by themselves. The puddled water on the runway provides fishtails behind us that are visible in the side-view mirrors. We slow to a crawl in about 6,000 feet and turn onto the flooded taxiway. Thank God, we are alive!

Although physically drained and wallowing in our own sweat juices, there is a feeling of exhilaration. I turn the heat to full cold and watch the canopy fog up. I then wipe it with my sticky wet gloves and enjoy the cooling change. We taxi into the tarmac area adjacent to the water tower, which is not visible under these conditions. The tower is 150 feet high! I think, so much for the 1,500 foot ceiling!

The rain is pounding the planes so intensely we can't open the canopies and exit. We sit there for forty-five minutes waiting for the rain to subside. No sense in ruining the cockpits—we'll need them tomorrow. The wait allows me time for a thankful prayer!

The lobsters notwithstanding, we decide that we have enjoyed enough flying for one day. It is almost noon. The O club will be opening in a short while and will have two very thirsty visitors for the balance of the day. Since we don't have additional clothes, the club officer graciously grants the two Marine lunatics permission to eat and drink in our sweat-drenched flight suits. By the time we have concluded both chores early that evening, our flight suits have dried to their usual perma-damp condition—still smelling like old socks, however. We have enough beer in us that it really doesn't bother us—not so sure about the other patrons. However, nobody says anything, and we are assured that we are most welcome anytime at K. I. Sawyer AFB.

The base was closed in 1996.

The lobsters wait until the next day when we enjoy an uneventful flight to Brunswick. The lobsters are loaded into the tanks and flown back to Cherry Point to meet their fate. The lobsters go comatose from the cold and lack of oxygen at altitude. They don't seem to mind the ride. When they hit the boiling water it becomes a different story! I wish that I could say that I learned the lesson of a lifetime, but unfortunately, I would repeat some of the same mistakes a year later in Japan. Fortunately for me, there was once again, a happy ending! I'm convinced my guardian angel is an aviator!

What is the definition of insanity?

CHAPTER 6

The Story Of Captain Jack Kennedy
A Tragedy

THE EARLY SPRING OF 1964 had its moments. March 3, 1964, is one that has stayed inside of me for almost fifty years. It's difficult to tell.

As background, I indicated earlier that in the pilot training cycle there are forks in the road. They are designed to allow young trainee pilots to be evaluated as to their flying skills and sent down the path toward naval aviator wings that seem to suit them best. Some fighter jocks assume the hubris of *Top Gun* and think less of a pilot who hasn't followed the jet pipeline. I absolutely reject that faulty theory. As the Irish put it, "There are horses for courses." The annals of the wars in Vietnam are packed with tales of sacrifices and unbelievable acts of heroism by both helicopter and OE spotter pilots—matching or exceeding those of fighter and attack jockeys like myself. This is not false humility—this is the truth!

Captain Jack Kennedy was a case in point. He had been directed through the helicopter pipeline and was, by all accounts, an excellent helicopter pilot. The Marine Corps, however, in its infinite wisdom, decided that Jack Kennedy should be retrained in jets and deployed with VMA-225 to the Far East.

When you fly as a wingman on another pilot, you instinctively know whether that other pilot is up for the game. His every movement portrays his attitude and reveals his skill-set. Is he with the aircraft or is he behind it? Is he thinking and functioning at seven miles a minute or is he still at three miles per minute? If he is not with or ahead of the aircraft, it's simply a matter of time before he runs into trouble. That's the way it is.

With that brutal, frank analysis, let me set the stage.

Cherry Point has four runways that intersect in the middle to form an X. The active runways that run in four directions around the clock-face are each eight thousand feet long before you get to the middle area of the cross. Then there is another eight thousand feet that continues past the center apron. In short, Cherry Point has sixteen thousand feet of runway in four directions when you count the middle apron.

Now the sad tale.

It's midmorning. I have taxied out and am sitting in my A4 Skyhawk, in the "long position" in the middle of the cross, waiting for clearance to take off on the north half of the active runway. There are aircraft landing behind me and slowing down to pass through the midfield apron and return to their hangars. They have used only eight thousand feet or the first half of the available runway. I will use the other half on takeoff.

While waiting for my takeoff clearance (I can't remember where I was going), I'm listening to the usual voice chatter on the radio. This time, however, I recognize our "Charlie Echo" (CE) call sign and the voice of Captain Jack Kennedy entering the pattern at 1,000 feet to "break" and land.

Suddenly, Jack is yelling over the air:

"My nose cone came off, my nose cone came off!"

The panic in his voice was electric!

For some inexplicable reason, the latch holding the radar dome failed when he "broke" into the pattern and put three to four g's on the aircraft. However, despite the loss of the front radar dome, the plane is still flying and the engine still turning. This is an uncomfortable situation but certainly addressable.

The emergency procedure is to level the wings, climb to 10,000 feet, and check the aerodynamics of the plane without the radar dome. Then, if satisfied that the problem is contained and the plane is flyable, return to a high station—10,000 feet directly over the runway markers—and commence a descending left turn until you land. At that altitude, it should take two or more 360-degree turns before you run out of air.

Here is where Jack has fallen behind the aircraft—he is functioning at two miles per minute instead of seven miles. As I sit there and listen, he declares an emergency—correct decision—and then he makes the decision to land the aircraft without climbing or testing it. Bad decision! I'm dumbfounded as I strain my neck to turn around and watch Jack land. He is FAB—"fast as a bastard"—and slams the A4 onto the runway.

It is the only way to get it there since it is so fast that it hasn't finished flying. In doing so, he apparently cracks the nose wheel rim, which sits directly below the pilot's seat. The violent landing and the subsequent wheel vibrations must have convinced him that the plane was really in bad shape and it distracted him from reducing power or even shutting down the engine. Remember, he has at least twelve thousand more feet of runway remaining in front of him!

As his plane approaches the center cross area with the other eight thousand feet left, it has barely slowed down. Then everything seems to go into slow motion. I watch in horror as the canopy blows off the aircraft as a precursor to an imminent ejection. I see the ejection seat start up the rails right in front of me—no more than one hundred yards away. The seat rotates once as he separates from it with the chute starting to deploy. Unfortunately, the A4 ejection seats do not have zero altitude and airspeed capability. He simply does not have either enough airspeed or altitude for the chute to flare, and he hits the ground directly in front of me with the chute still streaming.

I shut down my aircraft, safe the ejection seat, open the canopy, unhook my flight gear, all in about twenty seconds, and jump down to the ground by swinging on the refueling probe. I race the short distance to Jack and release his parachute, which has billowed and is dragging him across the tarmac. I sit on the ground and cradle his head in my arms. He's unconscious and blood is streaming from under his helmet and onto our flight suits. I speak but there is no answer. His eyes are open but frozen in a blank stare. With the brisk wind swirling around us, time seems to stand still.

In a few long minutes, the emergency ambulance is there. Together we lift Jack onto a stretcher. I ride with him in the ambulance to the base hospital and he's taken directly into the operating room. I wait outside until his wife, Agnes, also a Marine captain, arrives. There isn't much to say.

Jack Kennedy was pronounced dead shortly thereafter. I think, how sad that in less than five short months, America would lose two Jack Kennedys—the president of the United States and then my fellow Marine.

The irony of the story, if there is one, is that when Jack and the seat exited the aircraft, the center of gravity shifted aft and with the power inexplicably still on, the plane took off again on the unused portion of the runway and flew three miles before finally crashing in the woods.

It was a tragic, unnecessary loss of a good pilot and a great Marine. Some desk jockey somewhere had decided that he or she knew better than the instructors in the training command. That desk jockey was wrong.

This was my first up-front-and-personal experience with tragedy and death in the Marine Corps. Unfortunately, it wouldn't be my last.

Semper Fi, my friend.

CHAPTER 7

Okinawa–New York—1964

It's Thanksgiving Day, 1964, and the squadron has deployed from Iwakuni to Kadena Air Force Base on Okinawa for special operational training. We are due to be here for a week and then back to Japan for Christmas. At this time Okinawa is still part of the Ryukyu Islands and not Japan proper.

At about noon, Col. Baker comes looking for me and informs me that he has been notified that my father, Frank, has had a serious heart attack and is in the Methodist Hospital in Brooklyn. Although information is still sketchy, he immediately authorizes emergency leave for me. One of the other guys in the squadron searches transportation options back to the States. The initial news is not good. If I wait for military transport, there is nothing leaving until after the holiday weekend and that would be a hopscotch arrangement across the Pacific on a space-available basis.

They discover that a Northwest Airlines 707, Flight 7, will be stopping at NAS Naha, the civilian terminal, at 5:00 p.m. en route to New York from Hong Kong. Although the time is short, less than three hours by then, my squadron mates have me packed and delivered to the commercial side of Naha Airfield in time to board the flight. My emergency leave papers have been cut and the reservation confirmed. I have a seat to New York.

With a last minute scramble to get ticketed and onboard, the plane departs on time in the late afternoon, Thanksgiving Day, and heads for Tokyo to refuel. It is early evening when we set down in Tokyo. I manage to deplane and shove some food into me—all the time thinking about my dad. I'm the only child, and our family of three is a close-knit unit. I never considered any one of us not being there!

About 10:00 p.m. we depart Tokyo and head for Seattle, ten hours away. It will be a long, thoughtful flight for me with the unknown waiting at the far end. My mind drifts back to my earlier years. Actually, I had a brother, Terrence, who was a few years younger than me and died just after childbirth. In later years I would reflect on how difficult a time it must have been for my mother and father. They never discussed the loss with me.

Looking out the window, I remember again how close we are as a family. How, when I was young, I would wait at the living room window watching for my father to turn the corner of Church Avenue and Stratford Road in Brooklyn on the way home from work. All those Saturdays when the Stock Exchange was open half-day, and my father would take me into work with him. We always rode the first car on the subway so I could stare into the darkness of the tunnel and watch the changing lights. Now, I stare out of the plane into the same darkness and watch the wingtip lights instead. I think how much those happy days meant to me.

I think about our first journey to Ebbets Field to see the Brooklyn Dodgers. What a thrill for a seven year old. It is a very long journey across the Pacific, but it gives me time to reflect.

The light comes up about two hours out of Seattle, and we finally arrive in late morning local time.

The airplane rests on the ground for the usual maintenance items and refueling, and we re-board the same aircraft and are back in the air by early afternoon.

Northwest still served lunch in the cheap seats at that time. The three-hour flight goes quickly and soon we are at the gate in Minneapolis. The layover is a short one, and I deplane only to make a phone call to New York and check in. I'm informed that Judy and our three-week-old baby, Diane, are arriving from Iowa at LaGuardia shortly. I'm getting anxious to see them all.

Soon we are back in the air, bound for Kennedy Airport (no longer Idlewild) on the last leg.

I remember the first time that my parents, Grace and Frank, met Judy in November 1961. They fell in love with her and remained so until they each passed. Judy was the daughter that my mother and father never had.

I will never forget my father's one serious admonition to me. When we were about to get married, he told me in the sternest terms I ever experienced from him, "Son, you take care of Judy as long as you live. She is a wonderful girl and is now your responsibility, and I want you to promise me that." In my imperfect way, I have tried to live up to his dream these past fifty-plus years.

There were so many other thoughts that careened through my head in those long hours in the air. The ones I've remembered are the important ones.

At 10:00 p.m. New York time, still Thanksgiving Day for me (we gained a day en route), I exit the same aircraft I had boarded some twenty-eight hours earlier in Okinawa. I'm met at the plane by my mother and Judy. We head immediately to the hospital to see my father. By this time the doctors had managed to stabilize him and, fortunately, his heart attack was not as severe as initially thought. He recovered over the next several weeks.

When Dad is well on his way to recovery, Judy, baby Diane, and I head to Iowa for Christmas. It's a great respite from the hectic days in New York, and I'm anxious to see the three other children, Tommy, Teri, and Linda. I spend about a week in Iowa with all of us together and Judy's family, whom I love. Unfortunately, the clock is ticking and on St. Stephen's Day, the day after Christmas, I say my good-byes and head back to Japan to rejoin the squadron. The next ten months away are a suspense-filled time for the family, indeed. How Judy managed four children under the age of three, I will never fully understand—particularly in light of events that lay ahead.

Judy and I have never been apart at Christmastime in the fifty-three years we have been together!

Little did I know that my father would survive this episode but be gone forever on Halloween night 1969—less than six years later. We still miss him!

CHAPTER 8

Cubi Point To Iwakuni

IT'S A BEAUTIFUL SUNDAY MORNING in the Philippines. We have been deployed to NAS Cubi Point for about a month. Two of our A4 Skyhawk fighter jets are due to be flown back to our home base at Iwakuni, Japan, for badly needed maintenance checks.

Two nights earlier, the annual ritual of celebrating the Marine Corps birthday had been rudely interrupted by the Navy officer of the day when he "closed" the bar—at 9:00 a.m. the following morning. It was not an easy chore getting a bunch of Marines down from the rafters. That bar is now enshrined at the Aviation Museum in Pensacola, Florida.

First Lieutenant Bobby Newsom and I are designated to fly the two A4s home. I'm leading the flight and file a flight plan for Naval Air Station Naha on the Island of Okinawa, about two-thirds of the way to Japan. We will land, refuel, and continue on to mainland Japan.

The flight line is quiet—not a surprise on a Sunday morning. Everyone must be at church!

The early morning air is broken by the sound of the two auxiliary power units screeching to a start. At full power they are louder than the airplanes.

After the perfunctory plane inspections, Bobby and I climb the ladders and are strapped into our seats by the plane captains. When comfortable, I give the hand signal for external air power. The rush of air to the engines bellows and the rpms begin to climb. As the needle passes 5 percent rpm, I slide the throttle around the shut-off detent and wait for the igniters to spark the fuel. There it is, the familiar throaty roar of engine ignition. The rpms slowly inch upward. When the needle crosses the 45 percent mark, I give the power-off signal to the plane captain and the external air is disengaged. The needle continues to climb and settles at 60 percent idle. The vibrations and the low rumble have now been replaced with the higher pitched whine of the turbine

I reach back on my right side and push in the circuit breakers, and all the instruments jump to life. Needles are spinning, gyros caging, and the radio is crackling in my ears.

Placing the mask over my mouth and nose and fastening it onto my helmet, I eagerly suck in the cold, refreshing 100 percent oxygen. After a few deep breaths any cobwebs that I had from the night before disappear. The mask has an integrated hot microphone so my breathing echoes in my ears. Keying the mic, I check in with the tower. Our flight plan is confirmed, and we are cleared to taxi. I look over at Bobby, we give each other the thumbs-up, and then, with our thumbs pointing outward, signal for the wheel chocks to be pulled. Adding some power, I move forward and he follows me down the taxiway.

We launch just past 0900, turn to the north and climb to 35,000 feet for the journey. The weather is clear as we fly up the western side of Luzon. The Philippines are beautiful. Heavy, dense foliage covers most of northern Luzon, interspersed with small farms closer to the coastline. We leave Luzon behind and set out over the Pacific Ocean. About forty-five minutes over the sea, we can see the mountains of Taiwan in the far distance off our left side.

Approaching Okinawa, the weather report is terrible—rainy and low ceilings as a cold front moves through the area. I had checked Iwakuni weather before takeoff and it was clear. The front had already passed. It is a beautiful wintery day in Japan.

I check our fuel state and calculate that if we climb a bit, we will have enough fuel to make the journey nonstop. I refile the flight plan for Iwakuni, and we climb to 39,000 feet and continue northward. All is well as the weather front below falls behind us. We are now on a familiar route segment as we pass alongside the east coast of Kyushu, the main southern island. Having made this journey between Okinawa and Iwakuni a half-dozen times, the sights are familiar.

We begin our descent over Kagoshima—pulling the power back to idle and essentially gliding at minimum power to conserve fuel. Bobby is still sitting in position about one-quarter mile abeam and enjoying the scenery, even though we had seen it all before. The beauty of Japan is breathtaking.

As we descend below 20,000 feet, I look down at the Inland Sea and can see whitecaps on the surface. Seeing them from this altitude really gets my attention as they are rolling from west to east. In a moment of stark terror, I quickly realize that if I can see them from this height, the wind must really be whipping. Then I remembered the cold front had passed only a few hours before! I should have paid more attention in Cubi Point!

Passing through 18,000 feet, we are handed off to Hiroshima Control on a discreet Marine Corps Air Station Iwakuni frequency. I establish contact with Iwakuni Control and they give me the existing weather report, including the winds aloft and on the ground. My heart freezes! Iwakuni is calling winds from due west at thirty knots, gusting higher. This presents a major problem as the sole runway at Iwakuni runs north-south! The crosswind component limitation for A4s is fifteen knots! There is real trouble ahead!

By now we are passing 15,000 feet and in an inexorable descent. I quickly dig out the flight manual for all JASDF (Japanese Self-Defense) bases within reach. While landing at one of them would not present a problem, they all have single runways that are also oriented north-south. No solution there!

This search consumes time, altitude, and fuel—all rapidly diminishing assets. I check with Bobby and he reports six hundred pounds of fuel. I am showing eight hundred pounds. The gauge error for the

A4 is plus or minus six hundred pounds. Below that point, it could get very quiet very quickly if the engine quits.

I call Iwakuni Control and tell them we are coming in—we have no alternative. They direct us to switch to the tower frequency and when established, I request that the midfield arresting gear be activated. This type of gear is unique to Marine and Navy bases—it is not the typical overrun gear that stops aircraft from leaving the runway. The MOREST gear is ground-anchored arresting gear designed to stop aircraft in a fashion similar to a carrier. The cables, which normally rest flat on the runway, are now elevated by rubber stanchions. They are positioned at a height designed to snare the landing hook unique to Navy and Marine airplanes.

Since Bobby is now at four hundred fifty pounds and in a dire fuel state, I direct him to land first and I will follow immediately. I am at six hundred pounds! We will land to the south away from the city, in case there is a mishap or wave-off. We set up for a left downwind and Bobby turns onto the final approach with the wind in full force. The wind buffeting is throwing our A4s all over the sky. He lines up the airplane in a ten-degree crab into the wind along the right side of the runway.

Approaching the midfield with gear, flaps, and hook down, Bobby kicks the rudder to the left to realign the aircraft. The crosswind immediately pushes the plane to the centerline and he lands just short of the arresting gear. The hook grabs the wire and he rolls to a stop in three hundred feet—by this time the crosswind has pushed the plane all the way to the left side of the runway.

I'm turning on final when Bobby grabs the wire. Fortunately for me, Bobby Newsom is a great pilot. He clears the arresting gear immediately and fights the wind to get off the runway. By the time he is clear, the cable has been repositioned and I am coming up the right side of the runway. I kick the rudder, land, pick up the wire, and when it slams me to a halt, I'm looking eyeball to eyeball with a left-side runway marker. The aircraft is sitting on its left and front gear as the arresting cable starts to retract. As with Bobby, the arresting cable has prevented the airplane from flipping over in the severe crosswind. The benefit of unintended consequences!

When we clear the runway we're unable to taxi the aircraft—they continuously weathercock into the wind, and we are afraid of flipping them. Both planes are shut down and towed onto the flight line and secured.

While it was good to be home – safely, we debrief the flight to the Duty Officer and I reflect on my mistakes in allowing the situation to develop that put both of our lives and planes in jeopardy.

The squadron returns to Iwakuni later in the week, and I address the pilots as a group. With a sense of detachment from my actions, I take them through my flawed thought processes and share my feelings and conclusions in an attempt to prevent anyone else from making the same mistakes. While it was not my intention in giving the debriefing, Colonel Baker squashed a flight violation that had justifiably been pending since the incident.

Reflecting on my motivations over these many years, I do believe that the experience I had with the Jack Kennedy tragedy spurred me to share my mistakes on that day.

Never a dull moment at seven miles a minute!

Epilogue:

There were two A4 Skyhawks that had emerged from PAR (preservation and repair) maintenance and were due to be returned to the squadron. They were the replacement airplanes for the ones we had ferried up from the Philippines.

Two days after our harrowing arrival in Iwakuni, Bobby Newsom jumped on a C130 to NAS Atsugi on the outskirts of Tokyo. Lieutenant Newsom was a "check pilot" in our maintenance department and was qualified to evaluate the aircraft and certify them for return to the fleet—in this case VMA-225. I was not, so I remained at Iwakuni to await word of acceptance before traveling to Tokyo.

The day after his arrival, having inspected all that he could on the ground, Bobby scheduled a final "check flight" for the next day. To set the stage, in those days smog was a major feature of most major industrial cities, and Tokyo was no exception. This day, a typical one for Tokyo, the sun was shining down and visibility vertically was excellent. However, with the sun striking the smog, there was virtually no lateral visibility.

Bobby took off in the A4 he was checking and climbed out to a test area. In putting the plane through its paces, the hydraulic system warning light illuminated. In any aircraft this is a serious malfunction. All of the control surfaces and the landing gear are dependent upon hydraulic power. If the warning light is accurate, and there is a real problem, the system, under pressure, can purge itself of fluid very quickly and render the aircraft uncontrollable.

Not knowing whether the warning light was accurate or simply an electrical problem, Bobby declared an emergency and headed back to Atsugi. To maintain sufficient altitude for safe ejection, he leveled at 1,000 feet and searched for the runway. The navigation aids brought him quickly overhead the airport.

At his altitude, he could see straight down but not horizontally. Suddenly he spotted the runway directly below him and turned to make a landing. The gear, flaps, and speed brakes were deployed but he lost the runway while in his approach turn and descending. The natural reaction in that situation is to keep a bit more power and speed than usual—sort of an insurance policy! He continued to fly the familiar landing pattern, looking again for the runway. Suddenly the runway approach lights were directly below him, and he headed for the ground.

He managed to find the runway and land. However, the insurance policy was to extract its premium—very quickly! He landed almost at the midway point on the runway and was FAB—fast as a bastard—as the LSOs would note in their books.

The Japanese are not fools. Directly off the end of the runway about two hundred meters was a commuter rail line. It had been there before the runway, to be sure. In anticipation of some potential future disaster, the Japan Railway Authority decided to cover the tracks with a concrete overpass, creating a tunnel beneath it for the trains.

As Bobby screamed off the end of the runway—probably at 120 knots or so—the A4 settled in the two hundred meters before the track cover just enough to shear the landing gear, flaps, and external fuel tanks from the plane. The now-uncontrollable missile skidded across the tunnel and came to an abrupt halt in the middle of a rice field. The immediate halt, similar to a carrier trap, creates massive negative g's. Everything goes forward—including the pilot and the throttle. In this case, the crash also broke the back of the A4. The cockpit, forward of air intakes and engine, was fractured from the main fuselage and cracked open the main fuel tank, situated directly behind the pilot.

With the engine roaring at 100 percent rpm, fuel was being siphoned out of the ruptured fuel tank and into the engine intakes. This was not the designed way to fuel feed a jet engine! Bobby was semiconscious and slumped against the instrument panel.

Seemingly from out of nowhere, a Navy rescue helicopter was overhead immediately. They had scrambled when Bob had declared his emergency.

Without hesitation, a Navy rescue man was lowered on a steel cable to a point next to the cockpit. Although soaked in fuel from the ruptured tank, the rescue crewman stood over the cockpit, the live ejection seat beneath him, unhooked Lieutenant Newsom, and lifted him to safety.

The aircraft continued to run for twenty minutes until it ran itself out of fuel. Amazingly, there was no fire. Had there been fire, the story would have ended quite differently.

I was notified of the accident and immediately hopped the next C130 to Atsugi. I arrived the next day and headed for the Navy hospital. I walked into Bobby's room, and he was strung up in every direction. He had suffered two broken forearms, a broken leg, a broken foot, two black eyes, and innumerable aches and pains. I commiserated with him, and we discussed how he had dodged death twice in the last week.

Two days later I flew the other A4 back to Iwakuni. The squadron was returning in a few days from the Philippines.

Four months later First Lieutenant Bob Newsom rejoined VMA-225 in time for our deployment to Vietnam.

Ironically, after leaving the Marine Corps, Bob Newsom enjoyed a distinguished thirty-year career as a test pilot for Beech Aircraft in Wichita, Kansas.

CHAPTER 9

My Most Memorable Flight

IT'S A QUIET FRIDAY AT Marine Corps Air Station Iwakuni, Japan, in March of 1965. I'm off-duty for the weekend and looking for somewhere to go for Happy Hour – that drinking and social ritual of every red-blooded fighter pilot! One of my closest mates was First Lieutenant Ron Kleiboeker, and he is also free for the weekend. We quickly determine that neither of us has been up to Misawa Air Force Base in Northern Japan, so that's where we decide to go for the evening. We clear the airplanes with scheduling, grab a packet of fuel chits, and off we go.

Filing the necessary paperwork, we launch from Iwakuni just after noon. Climbing out, we head north, up the Inland Sea, past Hiroshima and directly for Osaka. I'm the flight leader so when we reach our assigned altitude of 30,000 feet, Ron takes his Skyhawk out to the perch position about a quarter mile abeam my right side, slightly aft and one hundred to two hundred feet above me. We are under the radar control of Tokyo Center, and it is a perfect late winter day. We can see forever.

Flying along the Inland Sea, sandwiched between the main island of Honshu on my left and Shikoku on the right, it is easy, even in 1965, to understand the industrial might and beauty of Japan. Below us is town after town that has already been rebuilt since WWII. Smokestacks from power plants and factories are spewing the evidence of the growth taking place. This is a giant reawakening and it doesn't take a genius to figure it out.

As Osaka passes below us and we head toward Tokyo, Mount Fujiyama and all its majestic charm appears on our left side. Despite having flown past and around it several times before, I'm still awed by its sheer symmetry and beauty. It is considered a sacred mountain and certainly the best-known symbol of Japan.

THE MAJESTIC MOUNT FUJIYAMA

It is only then that I realize I have unintentionally left my brand new Ricoh camera back in Iwakuni. It is to prove an unfortunate omission. Ron, however, has his camera and manages to snap this photo of me from his right-wing position.

We pass Tokyo and make the obligatory confirmation of altitude to the air controllers far below us. My plane is purring like a kitten as we turn slightly from northeast to a direct north, heading to Misawa about three hundred miles away. I have my plane on autopilot for altitude control. The directional aspect of the autopilot that controls heading never seems to work on the Skyhawk. Besides, the view is unlimited and a degree or so off-course one way or the other doesn't seem to matter.

About 120 miles north of Tokyo, I have my head down in the cockpit studying the landing approach plates for Misawa Air Force Base when suddenly Ron screams into his microphone and my earpiece:

"DASH 1—BREAK RIGHT, BREAK RIGHT!"

Without a second's hesitation I grab the stick, overriding the autopilot, and pull two g's into a right turn toward Ron—four g's would stall the aircraft at that altitude.

As I pull away to the right, looming into view is a JAL 707 flying directly into my airspace. In a split second we pass each other only a few hundred feet apart and on reciprocal headings. I watch in suspended animation and look into the passenger windows as we pass at a combined closing speed in excess of one thousand miles per hour. In that brief second or two I read the Japan Airlines logo and can see the passengers clearly—whether they or the crew ever saw me, we'll never know. I hope they did not.

Because Ron had been in the correct wing position out to my right side, he had the angle and elevation and was able to discern the contrails (or smoke) from the old engines on the 707. The early jet engines left a trail of unburned fuel in the form of black smoke, which morphed into contrails at this altitude due to the extremely cold temperature. Thank God. After a moment's delay, my hands start shaking, and I'm suddenly soaking wet in my flight suit. A near miss will do that every time.

These were the early days of radar control and coverage was not universal. Obviously, 120 miles north of Tokyo we had exceeded the effective radar range. Discussing the situation later, we guessed that the flight was inbound from the United States at a higher altitude and had just commenced its descent into Tokyo—still about one hundred miles ahead. It was probably just passing through 30,000 feet, descending to a lower altitude, and had not been alerted by Tokyo Center to our presence heading north. Had Ron not been alert, the results certainly would have ruined the day for a lot of folks, including myself.

With that episode behind us, we continue to fly onward to Misawa. With 175 miles left to go, at seven miles per minute, the rest of the journey goes by quickly. Wallowing in my own nervous sweat, I reflect on the near miss all the way to Misawa. Suddenly the interest in viewing the sights has waned a bit. We are on the ground in less than forty minutes.

Since it is a Friday night on a US Air Force base, Ron and I had stuffed civilian clothes into our baggage compartment. We always try to schedule our cross-country arrivals to allow a shower and change of clothes and "just-in-time" arrival for Happy Hour (discount drinks and hors d'ouvres) at the Officers Club. All Air Force clubs jump on Friday nights and Misawa is no exception. By the time we arrive, I have convinced myself that I deserve a beer or two for the near miss.

Ron and I have a half-dozen drinks between us, eat dinner in the club, and go to bed. I have scheduled an early morning launch on the next leg of our sightseeing journey. We are departing at 0800 on a VFR (Visual Flight Rules) flight plan to take advantage of the clear weather in northern Japan. Little do I realize that I will be embarking on the most visually memorable flight of my entire aviation career.

It's still dark when we arrive at the flight line the next morning. Saturdays are usually quiet. After the routine preflight check, we climb into our cockpits and start the engines. First light has just broken on the eastern horizon. Tuning up the radios, I check in with ground control and receive our VFR clearance. The route we have chosen, since the weather is absolutely clear, is to launch and head across the water for the city of Sapporo at the southern end of Hokkaido—the northernmost island in the Japanese chain.

With clearance in hand, we taxi out and take off to the northwest. The whole sky is now light but still some time to go until sunrise. With a minor adjustment, we head directly to Sapporo. We climb to 16,000 feet, just below radar-control airspace, and settle in for the flight of a lifetime.

Quickly passing Sapporo, we let down and turn up the west shoreline of Hokkaido. Leveling at 1,000 feet, I notice a single railroad track winding its way along the rocky coastline. It is reminiscent of the rugged California coast along Big Sur.

The sun is now rising above the mountains of Hokkaido that lay to our right side and loom above us. I think, this is truly "The Land of the Rising Sun!" We are cruising at 420 knots, taking in all the beauty of this fantastic country. Over to our left there is a low layer of fog sitting atop the water off the coast, again similar to the Monterey Peninsula or around San Francisco. We are cruising the seam between the rugged mountains of Hokkaido and the lower fog at sea. After about twenty minutes of following the railroad track north, about twenty miles offshore, there looms a smaller Mount Fujiyama—a perfect snow-covered conical mountain peak thrusting up through the fog and rising above us to about 3,000feet. Sheer majesty! I'm awestruck. It's not on any of the flight maps that I have studied. It is a magical moment that I can't seem to forget some fifty years later. When I researched it later, I discovered it was the religiously symbolic Mount Rashiri on the island of IO (pronounced ee-oh).

As we fly past IO, I can see early morning smoke rising ahead of us in the distance. We quickly come upon the sleepy town of Wakkanai on the northwestern tip of Japan. The smoke is coming from the chimneys of the quaint houses now below us. We circle the town a few times and then head east along the north coast of Hokkaido.

Turning east over Wakkanai, twenty miles off my left wing we can plainly see the start of the Sakhalin Island chain—stolen from Japan by the Russians at the end of WWII. I imagine that we are lighting up all the Russian radar sites in that part of the world. I seriously doubt that they would envision us on a sightseeing tour. However, we stay very close to the Hokkaido shoreline! No need to start WWIII on a quiet Saturday morning. Besides, we have no ammo!

The northern shoreline is sheer rugged beauty devoid of any towns. So, with most of the beauty behind us and an eye on the fuel gauge, we turn south and hopscotch the snow-capped mountains of Hokkaido on our way back to Misawa. This is 1965, and the few ski resorts that we spot are not well developed at this time. It will change dramatically in a few years.

We arrive back at Misawa after an elapsed flight time of one hour, forty minutes.

While the ground crews are refueling our aircraft, Ron and I grab a late breakfast in the canteen. When the planes are ready, we file a flight plan back to Iwakuni and head home. It is now Saturday and we again make sure that we arrive "home" just in time for Hour. Happy

Looking back, that was simply the most memorable and enjoyable flight of my flying career. And no camera to prove it

CHAPTER 10

Cebu On A Special Day—1965

IT'S AN OVERCAST DAY IN the Philippines. Our squadron, VMA-225, has been recruited for a four-plane division of A4 Skyhawk jets to fly down to Cebu City and participate in the 1965 celebration of Philippine Aviation Week. This is a big event throughout the Philippines. It's the twentieth anniversary of the end of WWII.

There will be military celebrations in the town of Cebu and a local flight demonstration. At the time, the Philippines was still very much in the orbit of the United States, and our part of the celebration is essentially a show of support and camaraderie. The fast jet, low-level flyby by the Air Force and the Marine Corps will be the highlight of the show. We are scheduled to fly up the main street of Cebu City at high noon.

The American part of the "air-show" is to consist of two four-plane divisions of aircraft—a contingent of US Air Force F-105s flying out of Clark Air Force Base and us, a Marine Corps flight of four A4 Skyhawks from Naval Air Station, Cubi Point.

Major Don Gillum is the division leader and, despite dour weather reports from Cebu, about three hundred miles south of Cubi Point, he decides to launch the mission.

In our preflight briefing, we review the sectional maps of the Cebu area that give us an accurate description of the terrain below. Cebu City sits on the southwest coast of the island and had three-thousand-foot mountains to its north and open sea to the south and west. This attention to the ground features is second nature to us and will shortly prove invaluable.

After starting our engines, we taxi out in single file. The runway at Cubi Point is not wide enough for multiple plane launches so we take off in single file. Major Gillum leads us into the air heading west to the sea and when clear of the mountains, commences a climbing left-hand turn. He is careful to stay below the cloud cover until the rest of us join up in formation. A few minutes later, with everyone in position, the lead gives the head nod for full power and the four aircraft surge up and into the clouds. The clouds are layered so we break out around 5,000 feet and continue our climb to 35,000 feet. Again, we ascend through several thin layers of high cirrus all the way up. We never get "on top"—above everything.

We listen as Major Gillum checks in with Manila Control and they vector us southward to Cebu. At seven miles a minute, the distance goes by quickly. Before long we are given the local frequency and instructed to contact the Cebu Airport air controller.

As we dial in the Cebu frequency, the air is filled with transmissions from the Air Force flight of F-105s ahead of us. They are discussing over the air the fact that they are not able to locate a hole in the cloud cover beneath them. This poses a problem as the area is mountainous and there is no radar control on the ground to vector them down safely. There are no breaks in the cloud cover below them, no openings through which to descend visually.

The chatter goes back and forth between their flight leader and the ground controller, who is not only disappointed but increasingly frustrated at the situation. We all listen quietly. We have about one hundred miles to go before facing the same dilemma. However, the difference is that we have anticipated the problem and are convinced we have a solution. Time will tell.

As we commence our descent, the Air Force leader announces that they have reached their "bingo" (critical) point in fuel and are aborting their mission and returning to Clark Field. The disappointment in the controller's voice is evident. His air show and the expectations of thousands of spectators on the ground are now hanging in the balance.

I feel a rush of adrenaline and can sense the same among the other pilots—don't ask me how, it just happens. You can feel it in the air. Everyone sits up a bit straighter in his seat. Time to go to work!

We are descending through 10,000 feet and in loose formation—twenty to thirty feet between airplanes. Major Gillum is the lead and his wingman, number 2, is on his right side. I am number 3 and on the left side and my wingman, number 4, is on my left side. When and if the time comes for the air show, number 4 will slide under me and into the slot position below and behind number 1, forming a four-plane diamond formation for the flyby. By now, this is a fairly routine adjustment in the formation.

As we descend, it is getting darker between the layers and the cloud below us is solid at 3,500 feet. The Air Force leader had been correct—there is no visual break in the cover below us. Tension is rising. My heart rate quickens, and the sweat runs out of my helmet and down my facemask. Nerves are only partly to blame—I have once again turned on the heat to maximum before descent to avoid windshield fogging from the moist, cold air outside, and it is easily ninety degrees in the cockpit. A small price to pay to be able to see!

Before launching, we determined that the small airport at Cebu did not have sophisticated navigation equipment but it did have a high-frequency localizer transmitter—a throwback to the earlier days of aviation. Before takeoff we had all dialed the frequency into our secondary navigation radios. While the localizer signal continually emits a Morse code ID, it does not indicate distance. However, it will indicate station passage if we fly directly overhead. It is now time to watch the ADF needle.

As we skim along the cloud layer at 3,500 feet, Don aims us directly at the ADF transmitter—needles on the nose. At 420 knots the dark clouds beneath us give a real sensation of speed that is missing at altitude. I think that's why I love flying at low levels—cloud hopping in particular.

We all wait for station passage. Time seems to stop for a few minutes. No transmissions are allowed, as they will foul up the ADF navigation system. The mountain peaks are passing below us at seven miles a minute, hidden from view by the solid cloud layer below.

I watch as suddenly my needle loosely swings from right to left, slowly at first, and then it starts to spin. In about ten seconds, the needle stops spinning and points directly at my tail. That is the indication for station passage—we have just crossed over the Cebu Airport.

Watching his own needle swing and lock on his tail, Major Gillum immediately turns us to a southwest heading of two hundred ten degrees, a vector aimed to take us out to sea. After a minute or so, he motions his head back several times, a signal for us to reduce power. Pulling back on the throttle and pushing forward on the stick, we start down into the ominous dark clouds below us. Already in formation, visibility isn't a problem as the solid clouds whisk past. After what seems an eternity, we suddenly break into the clear at 1,500 feet with the dark blue sea below us. A natural sense of relief floods my body—we have made it.

Settling at 420 knots, Don commences a gentle left-hand turn to line up the city. We continue our descent and, as we come around to a north heading and level at 500 feet, Cebu City comes into view ten miles directly ahead of us. With a head nod I signal my wingman to slide into the slot position, and we all tighten up the formation to about ten feet from canopy to wingtip. The voice of the air controller says it all. He is ecstatic that we have continued our mission and punched down through the clouds. Now he will have the airplanes for his air show!

In a minute or so we cross the beach and are flying up the main *avenido* and directly overhead Cebu City. It is five minutes past noon—about five minutes late due to the diversion in the descent. Somehow that doesn't seem to matter very much to the air controller.

With fuel an issue this far from home, we make one sweeping, low-level pass and then the high mountains loom ahead of us. With a leader's nod to add full power, we commence a steep climb back into the clouds and head north to Cubi Point. Number 4 leaves the slot and slides back out to my wing position. After breaking clear of the clouds at 3,500 feet, Major Gillum wishes the Cebu controller a pleasant day, and we accept his never-ending words of gratitude.

Nurturing a deep sense of satisfaction and typical Marine pride, we are all hoping that the Air Force flight is still up on the local channel to hear the accolades from below. If they are, they remain silent!

Forty-five minutes later, we cross over the historic shell of Corregidor and enter the landing pattern for Cubi Point. We're on the ground ten minutes later. A very memorable mission accomplished.

ANECDOTE:

In 2015, at an Operation Smile gathering in Norfolk, I was introduced to the current Mayor of Cebu City. After the usual pleasantries, the Mayor asked if I had ever been to Cebu. In a coy fashion, I answered, "sort of," intending to pique his curiosity. He bit, and I told him I had been there in 1965 at 500 feet. He looked puzzled.

I mentioned that I was in a four-plane formation of Marine jets that had flown over the city for the twentieth anniversary of Philippine Aviation Week. With absolute recall, the Mayor told me he had been on the ground watching the show—he was seven years old at the time! It was that big of a deal for Cebu. It's a small, small world, indeed!

It also made me feel very old!

I have shared this story with the Mayor.

CHAPTER 11

Vietnam—TPQ-10 Night Mission

IT'S SUMMERTIME IN VIETNAM, HOT and humid everywhere. Chu Lai enjoys the ocean breezes flowing in from the South China Sea so despite the heat, it is almost livable. VMA-225 squats in tents near the beach—not a bad deal, considering where we are.

Every afternoon, we watch the thunderstorms build up along the mountain ridgeline that divides Vietnam in two. To the east lies the fertile lowland of rice paddies and most of the population. To the west of the mountain spine are the "highlands." These consist of a few population areas surrounding rubber plantations carved out of the steamy tropical jungle.

In July of 1965, the Ho Chi Minh trail coming down through western Vietnam and Cambodia had achieved prominence as the main north-south supply highway for the Viet Cong. Something had to be done to try to intercept the flow of men and munitions south.

Let's remember that we lived in the world of hard electronics in 1965. The exotic possibilities of weapons systems that used microprocessors and computer chips simply did not exist. They hadn't been invented yet. So the attempt to remotely control aircraft from the ground, although cutting-edge, was rudimentary at best.

THUNDERSTORM BUILDUP TO THE WEST

The first attempt by the Marine Corps was a system known as TPQ-10. It consisted of an air controller sitting in an electronics trailer on the ground somewhere within communications distance from the aircraft. At a prearranged point in the air, the TPQ-10 operator would take control of the airplane and fly it to a specified point and trigger a bomb release. Today it would be child's play—in 1965, it was still a mystery.

That sets the stage for the following story—a mission that I repeated on five occasions.

There's a Group briefing on the buildup of the Ho Chi Minh Trail and the rationale behind the missions assigned by Saigon over the next two weeks. Every squadron is to share a role in the interdiction of movement along the Trail every night—when it is assumed the major activity is taking place. Starting at 2200 every night through to 0400, Marine Air Group 12 will have an aircraft on station over the highlands every hour to coordinate with the TPQ-10 operator on the ground and drop bombs. That is the assigned mission that includes VMA-225, my squadron. So I'm in the rotation for sure.

To avoid total confusion on the flight line and avoid double staffing, each squadron takes a turn on different nights. With two squadrons stationed at Chu Lai, it means we will fly missions every other night. The schedules from Group are posted downstream and the squadrons then assign the missions in the morning for the flights that night. The theory is the pilots scheduled to fly will get rest during the daytime. The reality is that the pilots assigned will watch the thunderstorm buildup all day—knowing that sixty-five-thousand-foot storm cells don't go away at night just because it gets dark!

Nothing strikes fear into a pilot's heart more than a thunderstorm—period!

I am assigned the 0200–0300 slot over the target area this evening, or is it morning? The area of interest is about 120 miles southwest of Chu Lai near the town of Ban Me Thuot, in the middle of the rubber plantations. Normally it takes about twenty minutes to get there but tonight will be different. After takeoff I will have to refuel and then pick my way through the thunderstorms to get to the highlands. This diversion will take about forty minutes. I set my launch time for 0120 and wait and watch.

After throwing down some canned "B" rations (that's "C" rations in bigger cans) at the chow tent, I head back to my tent to try to get some sleep. It is still light until 2100 but I manage to sneak in about four hours of fitful sleep.

My cot is on sand and I can never get it set right. It always seems to move when I turn over and tilt one way or the other.

Then there are the night sounds—strange noises mixed with the whine of the nearby power-starting units, followed by the dull roar of the airplane engines lighting off. It's strange how you can count the number of engine starts while sound asleep, knowing that in a few hours, yours will be one of them.

By 0030 I am up and moving. The rest of my tent is asleep. Only one other pilot in my tent is scheduled this evening, and he was on the early shift. We will be passing each other somewhere along the route.

MY LITTLE BIT OF HEAVEN

Climbing into my ever-damp, smelly flight suit, I grab my helmet bag, mask, and lap pad and quietly head for the operations tent. The climb over the hill and through the sand takes about ten minutes. For night operations, the tent is illuminated in an eerie red light to preserve whatever night vision the pilots might have. I check in, get the relevant radio frequencies and the identification codes in a handout, and then head for the flight line. I will get my aircraft assignment there.

Five minutes later I'm at the flight line and talking with one of my favorite plane captains, Corporal Marty Halpin. I review the maintenance book to see if the airplane has any particular problems with the engine systems or the radios. They all have a history of radio problems in these conditions—I just want to know beforehand which ones they are.

Marty and I walk down the flight line to the revetment that holds my aircraft. Marty is one of those Runyonesque characters from New York—he is typecast and will talk the ear off a brass monkey! While he is talking, I'm stealing glances to the west just to see if I can detect any break in the thunderstorm line. It is pitch-black, and I can't see a thing! I don't know whether moonlight would be good or bad. It is academic; there isn't any!

When we get to my plane, I walk around it with a red flashlight and check the obvious. Then I closely check the bomb racks. I have a full load of twelve, five-hundred-pound bombs, six on each rack. I will be lifting off with a light fuel load and six thousand pounds of ordnance, plus the usual complement of twenty-mm cannon shells. In this heat, even with two JATO (jet-assisted takeoff) bottles strapped on, I can only carry a full load of either fuel or bombs, but not both! In the sixty-three missions I flew in Vietnam, I never lifted off with a full fuel load. The ammo came first. I refueled in the air on every mission.

I climb into the cockpit and Marty helps me strap in. First the "G-suit", a nylon girdle that encompasses the lower abdomen, the thighs and the calves. It inflates to pressurize those areas to offset the effects of increased 'g' or gravity pressures that drain blood from the upper body due to aerobatic maneuvers, arrested landings or catapult takeoffs.

Then the parachute harness and radio cords are fastened and finally, when all that is done, I arm the ejection seat by flipping up the lever behind my head. I am ready to go flying!

With the oxygen flowing, I snap my mask into place and contact ground control for permission to start my engine. Permission granted, I give Marty the rotating index finger for engine start. He has already lit off the auxiliary power unit and plugged the air supply into my engine. With a flip of a switch, the compressed air flows and the engine starts to rotate. At 5 percent rpm, I come around the off-detent with the throttle, and at 15 percent I feel ignition and the dull roar as the engine accelerates. At 45 percent I give him the APU cutoff signal, and my engine continues on its own to 60 percent idle rpm. The exhaust temperature needle rises almost to its limit and then drops into range as the engine rpms increase and the combustion normalizes.

I push in the circuit breakers for the radios and the nightlights. I always enjoyed night flying. The navigation needles and gyros spin at first and then lock into position. All the gauges glow in the red light. It's a shame this sense of eeriness is lost in the daytime.

I have my clearance to taxi and my flight plan in hand, or better yet, on my kneepad, which is strapped to my left knee. My right knee provides an armrest for my "stick" arm. Chocks out and I slowly exit the revetment, which consists of fifty-five-gallon barrels filled with sand.

I turn right and head down the very narrow and wavy taxiway heading south. The taxiway lights are beneath my wing tips but provide all the guidance I need to get where I am going.

At the end of the taxiway I turn right and stop. The two JATO bottles on my closed speed brakes are armed. It is too dangerous to arm the JATO rockets on the flight line—stray electronic surges could ignite them and cause mayhem. They are solid-fuel rockets that provide three thousand pounds of thrust apiece for six seconds, enough to accelerate the A4 to takeoff speed on the shortened thirty-five-hundred-foot runway. Now I'm armed and ready!

I have the green light to go. Taxiing onto the aluminum-matting runway, I stand on the brakes and run the engine to 80 percent. I give a final but thorough check of my instruments—all look good—flick the wingtip lights, and then turn them off as I start my roll. Ten seconds into my roll, at about 80 knots, I push the ignition button on the throttle for the JATO to ignite. It goes off with a roar, and I am pressed into the back of my seat. The airplane accelerates rapidly in the six-second burn and when they finish burning, I am at 160 knots and rotating the nose up to go flying.

Once airborne, I retract the wheels and flaps and turn out to sea. About a mile offshore, I pickle the JATO bottles into the sea. They have served their purpose and Thiokol will be happy to replace them.

I leave Chu Lai departure control and check in on the tanker frequency. The C130 has been orbiting at 20,000 feet all evening to refuel the A4s after takeoff. I turn my lights back on at altitude so they can see me and help guide me to them. This is routine by now, so finding each other isn't a problem. I spot the tanker's lights about the same time he spots me. He is in a racetrack pattern, and I approach him from 1000 feet below, for everyone's safety. I pick up the closing vector and start to slide closer to him. Then suddenly his wing lights give way to the huge hulk of the C130 outlined in the starlight. Pulling back on the power to stabilize myself, I slide into position just below and behind him. The refueling drogue is already extended and staring me in the face—it's a busy gas station tonight and always a welcome sight!

Settling in behind him, I slowly add power and move forward toward the refueling "basket" at the end of the eighty-foot hose. The refueling probe on the A4 is on the right side just in front of the canopy. The concept is to drive my right foot into the basket and move it forward so it locks onto the end of the probe. I manage that on the first try. Then I watch the refueling lights on the refueling pod—red for "stay away," amber for "plug in," and green for "you are full"—time to depart. Since I am topping off, the refueling time is short, and I am soon on my way. A hearty "thank you," and I am gone.

Now the flight really begins. All that has happened so far is to get me to where I have to be—overhead Ban Me Thuot at 20,000 feet at 0200 hours!

With a full fuel load and all the ordnance on the wings, I struggle to get the A4 to 30,000 feet as I head southwest to my target area. I need as much altitude as possible to allow me to pick my way through the thunderstorms that lie ahead. It is a moonless night but the stars do help outline my challenge. I have switched on the small air-to-ground radar. The screen flickers with its green outline of objects ahead. I've oriented the radar to my flight path in a vague attempt to identify thunder cells hidden in the storms. The surreal glow and sweep of the cursor gives me a false sense of security because, from experience, I know that it really doesn't work very well. But anything that makes me feel better is very welcome up here.

Ground control has reasserted control over me once I departed the tanker. To confirm my location, I'm told to "ident" or activate my code transponder in a fashion that illuminates it on their radar. We confirm that I am who I say I am, and they give me a vector to follow—not that any other sane person would be up here in the middle of the night! The heading is their best guess—looking at the thunderstorm activity on their more powerful ground radar—how to steer me through the wall of weather in front of me. I am all ears.

The massive clouds are getting closer by the minute. My instrument lights reflect the eerie red glow off the inside of my canopy. I love the feeling. It's like being in a cocoon. Suspended animation— no sensation of speed. The transmissions have gone quiet now. There is only one other airplane in the air and he is heading my way with no lights on either. His aircraft is lighter and assigned a higher altitude, so nothing to worry about. It's my squadron mate, Jim Saunders, and he is heading home and back to his cot. We pass in the ether sight unseen.

Adrenaline is starting to rush now. My ears pick up every possible engine sound, every tick that seems out of the ordinary is magnified. My lifeline now is the engine. I'm over one hundred miles into enemy territory and if there is aircraft trouble, I am in trouble. This is not the place to bail out. It would be a very long walk home. It might take years.

I'm entering the line of thunderstorms now. At 30,000 feet, they tower over me—the size is beyond description. They must top out around 60,000 feet. My small radar and the ground controller, who has come back to life, both indicate a path between two massive cells. I turn ten degrees to the left and intend to split them. The lightning has one benefit—it illuminates my path between the two storms. Most of the lightning is below my altitude. The clouds burst with the glow of it, seeming to light from within, self-contained, like the inside of a frosted light bulb. I skirt the two clouds, mild bumping but nothing severe. In about ten minutes I can see clearly ahead with the starlight. I'm leaving the line of thunderstorms behind me now as I head farther south and west. My heart rate slows down, and I relax a bit.

With about forty miles to Ban Me Thuot, ground control instructs me to contact them on another frequency. I comply and check in with their TPQ-10 controller who is lodged in a van somewhere below me. Hopefully he is well hidden.

He tells me to descend to 20,000 feet, the release altitude for the bombs. In a few minutes I am steady at 20,000 feet and he then instructs me to arm my autopilot for his TPQ-10 radar. I comply and then he tells me to release my grip on the stick—an unnatural move for sure. As I do and tell him, he engages his gear and takes control of my airplane. I feel him engage the autopilot—a weird and uncomfortable situation, but at least I have 20,000 feet of air beneath me to correct any mistakes.

The controller then gives me a few mild turns to confirm his control. No problems so far. He then declares that we are commencing a bombing run in one minute and to arm my bomb racks. He wants a single release from each wing station, two bombs at a time. This will mean six runs. I have plenty of fuel so I am not worried; I'm rather more curious than anything.

I'm sitting in almost complete darkness, save for starlight and the red glow of my instrument lights, with some stranger 20,000 feet below and miles away who has control of my aircraft. There are no reference points; it's like I am flying in an inkwell. He begins the countdown to release then suddenly I feel the release of the two five-hundred-pound bombs. They're on their way—lord knows where. After a moment or so, the controller turns me around in a thirty-degree turn—very disconcerting for sure. My hand is surrounding the stick just in case! As I look out into the darkness, I see the two telltale flashes as the bombs hit the jungle. They have proximity fuses designed to explode at one hundred feet above the ground.

We continue this exercise for five more bombing runs. The only thing that I know for certain is that the bombs reach the ground and explode as advertised. Whether we hit anything besides the ground or disrupt any Viet Cong movements is beyond my pay-grade. After thirty minutes under TPQ-10 control, I'm instructed to take back control of my airplane, safe my weapons, or what's left of them, and head home. I exchange greetings with my fellow Marine and head for Chu Lai, 140 miles away.

As with Jim Saunders before me, I contact the air controller and climb to 35,000 feet for the ride back to Chu Lai. Soon the storms are in front of me, and I once again manage to pick my way through the "light show" and emerge safely on the coastal side. I reach down and turn off the radar. The green glow is starting to bother me now. I find myself staring at it, transfixed. It'll do me no further good in getting safely on the ground tonight.

In about fifteen minutes I'm lined up for a straight-in approach to Chu Lai. I keep the exterior lights off for safety reasons—no need to tell the VC where I am when I'm this low to the ground.

The landing lights at Chu Lai have been turned on for me—two thin strips along the runway. At one mile I drop the gear, flaps, and hook and report them down and locked. I'm cleared to land.

Due to the short runway, we have utilized the MOREST gear since our first missions, the carrier-style arresting cable strung across the runway about one thousand feet from the apron. It is designed to grab the arresting hook on the aircraft after some rollout. In addition, since Chu Lai has more runway than a carrier, the run-out length after snatching the hook is several hundred feet. This longer rollout reduces the stress on both the airplane and the arresting gear. Still, due to the sandy nature of the terrain, the constant jarring requires that the arresting gear be repositioned every two weeks or so.

I land on the aluminum matting and wait for the hook and cable to meet and bring me to a gradual stop. There it is, right on target. I reduce power to idle and after stopping, flick on my external lights to see where I'm going, retract the hook, and exit the runway at the midpoint. After taxiing in to the revetment, Marty is there to greet me. I watch for his command to shut down the engine and secure the seat and the radios.

I'm a bit early; it's only 0330. Off the oxygen now, as I climb down the ladder, I suddenly feel physically tired. The exhilaration of the flight has kept the adrenaline flowing. Now it's time for a fast debriefing and some real sleep.

In ten minutes I've finished the debriefing—not much to tell— then I cross the sand and straggle into my still and silent tent. Finding my little corner of civilization, I collapse on my still unbalanced cot but who cares! I'm asleep at 0400. Mission accomplished.

HOME SWEET HOME

ANECDOTE:

In the late 1970s and early 1980s, we spent most of the winter holidays in Aspen, Colorado.

During one of the Christmas periods, I forget which year, Judy, the children, and I went on a shopping spree on Christmas Eve. To wind up the evening, we stopped at one of our usual watering holes, Little Annie's bar. We were not strangers to the place.

The manager/owner, not sure which, was a hippie-looking guy named John. I called him Big John for no particular reason other than he was. For the past number of years, I had typecast Big John as a throwback to the Haight-Asbury district of San Francisco. With long hair, he looked the part.

On this particular night, I had decided to taste a few B52 shots for a change from my usual rum and diet Cokes. John was behind the bar and decided to join me. After a few drinks we began to chat in earnest. Before long, we moved to the topic to Vietnam to liven up the discussion a bit. I disclosed my tour in the Marine Corps as a badge of honor and in hopes of starting a debate—whiskey will do that to you!

Much to my surprise, Big John revealed that he was also a Marine and had served in Vietnam. Quickly we bracketed the timeframes for each of us. I disclosed that I was an A4 pilot, and he disclosed that he was a communications guy—in fact, he was a TPQ-10 operator. I almost fell off the chair. In discussing the dates of our tours, some fifteen years earlier, we discovered that we were both in-country from June–October 1965. While I was at Chu Lai, he was sitting in a trailer at Ban me Thuot!

Through the process of elimination, we determined that he had controlled several of my TPQ-10 flights over the plantation country. Needless to say, we celebrated well into the night, and I swore that I would never profile someone again—a vow that I have broken many, many times since.

CHAPTER 12

Vietnam—Helo Rescue Flight

It's a routine helicopter escort mission. Lieutenant Conrad "Ham" Hamilton and I launch from Chu Lai in the early afternoon and, after aerial refueling, proceed north toward the DMZ. We're to orbit overhead Tam Ky at 10,000 feet and wait to provide air cover for a Marine helicopter that is on a resupply run to outposts between Tam Ky and Da Nang. I have participated on similar missions at least twenty times before. Some were exciting; most were quiet.

I'm the lead aircraft, and we reach Tam Ky in about twenty minutes, which is ten ahead of schedule, and start a lazy orbit at 10,000 feet. I establish radio contact with our aerial convoy on the ground. He has encountered a delay and will be a few minutes longer. Not unusual as they have a lot of moving parts with which to contend.

About ten minutes into the orbit, a very tense voice cuts in on the Guard Channel—the emergency frequency that all aircraft monitor. It is the pilot of a "Huey" helicopter that has been shot down. He estimates his position as twelve miles southwest of the Da Nang Airfield in a rice paddy. They are taking small-arms fire from three sides and are trapped in the aircraft.

Although we're sixty miles north, it becomes obvious that we are the only aircraft available for assistance. I immediately tell the helicopter on the ground to stay put. They also have heard the transmissions and are aware that we are needed elsewhere and understand the situation completely.

We turn our A4s south and start to descend. Leaving the power up, we're going downhill at 480 knots toward Da Nang. At eight miles a minute, we cover the distance in less than ten minutes, while establishing radio contact on Guard Channel. By the time we pass Da Nang, we are at 1,000 feet and have slowed to 420 knots. Scanning the ground, we spot the wounded chopper in a rice paddy just off our left wing. I signal to pop the speed brakes and we commence a left-hand pattern around the paddy at 400 feet and 420 knots.

I tell Ham to "go hot" with our twenty-mm cannons. Ham drops behind me in a trail position and we establish a racetrack pattern above the downed helicopter. After a spotting run to look over the area, the Huey pilot on the ground tells us he's taking heavy fire from a house at the northwest corner of the field. I am next in!

At 420 knots and 250 feet, I'm staring into the windows of the house. With zero deflection on my gun-sight, on my first burst I follow the tracer rounds—every third—and watch where they impact. I'm a bit high on the target since we are so close. I adjust my gun-sight and eyeballs down a bit for the next rip. A little "Kentucky windage" is all that is needed!

I call "off" the target and Ham rolls in behind me. Turning sharply to my left, I start to come around again. Ahead of me, Ham has also given the house a blast and taken out the doorway, then he calls "off" and climbs to go around again. The Huey pilot says that we are drawing fire but there is no way to prove it or see it.

We then concentrate on the tree lines along the other three sides of the rice paddy. Following the spotting from the grounded Huey pilot, we rake the trees and manage to scatter whoever is firing at them.

Not knowing how long we will be needed on station, and to conserve ammunition, I tell Ham that we will alternate dummy runs with firing runs. As you would expect, after the first few hot runs, whenever the VC spot either of us rolling in, their heads go down whether we fire or not! Even with only two aircraft in the pattern, one of us is constantly pulling out and the other A4 starting to roll in—we keep the flight pattern very tight and in sight of the guys on the ground at all times.

Conrad and I are on target overhead for almost thirty minutes before a rescue helicopter shows on the scene. By that time we have shot-up the house and the surrounding woods fairly well. The remaining ground fire, as we're told by the pilot on the ground, is now sporadic, in particular when we are making a pass, hot or dummy.

A rescue chopper, another Huey, arrives and is orbiting above us. When the enemy fire slows down, he lands next to the downed one and lifts eight Marines to safety. They make a fast run to Da Nang to offload the wounded.

As the first rescue helicopter departs, a second Huey lands and retrieves the remaining crew. By the time they evacuate the balance, we are getting low on fuel. An hour of low-level work will chew up your gas. Fortunately, we had topped off when first launched and had been early into our mission.

About the time the last Huey is lifting off, a replacement flight of F4s launches from Da Nang to relieve us on station. In their enthusiasm, we watch as they scream past us at about 2,000 feet and 500 knots en route to somewhere. The F4 Phantoms at that time were air-to-air interceptors and not trained at low-level operations. Although that would change at a later date, I get great delight in calling them back to the crash site.

The VC are alerted to the downed helicopter, and by the time the crews are rescued it becomes obvious to them that we are low on fuel and ammunition. VC reinforcements have arrived, and it is necessary for the F4s to destroy the downed helicopter or what was left of it. It isn't worth any more casualties trying to salvage a shot-up bird.

As we leave, I head us back to Chu Lai, which is not a difficult feat as it lies about forty miles south and east of our position. We climb to 2,000 feet and virtually enter the landing pattern. When we land and taxi into the revetments, there is considerable excitement. As Marine pilots, we live to assist our fellow Marines on the ground and the ground crews also feel the tension. They monitor the radio waves all day, every day. Today they heard their own airplanes called into action and listened intently to every transmission.

After deplaning, Ham and I work our way through the sand and up the hill to Group Operations. This is usually routine but today everyone wants to hear the details. I fill out an "after action report" that relates every detail that we can remember. Little do I know that it was to become the basis for a recommendation for a Distinguished Flying Cross. I didn't think what we did deserve such a prestigious award. But needless to say, when later advised of it, I was proud of what we had done.

Apparently, since we couldn't verify that we had received enemy fire and we had not been hit, the DFC was downgraded to a single-flight Air Medal. It was my seventh Air Medal, and I was quite happy with that. With no false modesty, we did what we were trained to do and were proud to have been in a position to do it.

Mission accomplished.

CHAPTER 13

A Mismatch of Aircraft

VMA-225 HAD BEEN OPERATING AT Chu Lai for about two months when VMA-311 arrived. They had come in from the States directly and were flying an advanced version of the A4 Skyhawk—the A4E model. The principal difference in the two aircraft was the engine. While it was apparently more fuel efficient, it left a telltale trail of smoke from the exhaust pipe. This was essentially unburned fuel symptomatic of earlier versions of jet engines on commercial airplanes. Even an untrained eye could see the "echo" coming from miles away.

The operations planners at the Marine Air Group 12 decided that a sense of welcome and camaraderie would be best served by flying a combined mission. In essence, they called for a mixed foursome. Two A4Cs from VMA-225 and two A4Es from VMA-311 would fly together. No one considered the very different endurance characteristics of the two aircraft.

I was selected to lead the VMA-225 two-plane section and, in furtherance of the ecumenism of the mission, Lieutenant Colonel (L/Col.) "Stubby" Stender, the Commanding Officer of VMA-311, would lead the four-plane division. I might point out that VMA-225 had been operating in theatre for almost three months, day and night, and Lieutenant Colonel Stender and his squadron had arrived two days earlier! This mission was destined for trouble in River City! Never having had the pleasure of flying with Lieutenant Colonel Stender, I had a high level of apprehension.

82

We all attended the preflight briefing at MAG12, including the photo-op guys. The mission was to fly 120 miles south to a target location in the jungle and drop our bombs. There would be a full load of five-hundred-pound bombs and the usual twenty-mm cannon ammunition on each aircraft. We would be guided by a low-level OE spotter aircraft when we arrived in the target area.

The weather below 10,000 feet was dark and afforded reduced visibility. There were higher layers of clouds reported from 10,000 feet up to 35,000 feet. There was clearly no opportunity get "on top" to refuel. We would have to find the tanker between layers. As we had been operating in similar weather patterns day and night since arriving months ago, this would not a problem for us. For the new guys, it would prove to be a different story.

I had met Lieutenant Colonel Stender briefly upon their arrival two days before. He seemed a decent guy and typical of the squadron commanders at that time. Most had been WWII and Korea veterans and had their training, and whatever combat time they had, in F4U Corsairs or some other prop planes. Perhaps over the years they picked up some F9F time, straight or swept wing, but usually that was the limit of their jet time. That is until they became squadron commanders.

We had experienced the same phenomenon with Lieutenant Colonels Gillis and Baker. Although they had great flying experience, it was rarely at seven miles per minute until they got to the A4. In our case, Gillis didn't make the cut and Bob Baker did. However, Lieutenant Colonel Baker was a different guy—he really knew his limitations and would deal around them. He relied upon the other pilots in the squadron and was never afraid to kid about himself and seek advice when he felt that he needed it. I was privileged to have spent many hours with Colonel Baker and always marveled at his humility and frankness. He was always the first to laugh at himself. A great personality trait I have tried to take with me through life. In many ways, he was my father away from home.

Now for the mission!

With the briefing complete, we head to our respective flight lines and aircraft. The two squadrons are at opposite ends of the flight line but easily linked via the radios when ready.

During my preflight inspection, I give special attention to the bomb load I am carrying. An additional six thousand pounds of weight does affect the flying characteristics, and I want to make sure that all is well. The starter power unit is already screeching in the background.

I climb the ladder and slide onto my seat. Angelo Lemme, my plane captain, helps with the hookup of oxygen, radios, and the G-suit. These connections are located behind me and, with the exception of the G-suit, everything plugs into the ejection seat. The radio is integral with my oxygen mask.

It is early afternoon and very hot this time of year. The temperature and humidity are both locked at around ninety. My flight suit never quite dries, but it is my lucky one. Even I can smell myself from a distance.

Getting the order to light off, I give Angelo the start-up signal, and the familiar rush of air hits the engine. A few seconds later, it is time to bring the throttle around the stop detent and the igniters begin their clicking. I feel the telltale thump as the fuel ignites and the engine slowly accelerates to 60 percent idle. At 45 percent I give the "thumbs-out" disconnect signals for first the air and then the electrical hookups. Now, I am on my own. Lieutenant Ron Kleiboeker, my wingman, does the same two revetments away.

Down the flight line, Lieutenant Colonel Stender and his wingman are repeating the same ritual in their A4Es.

The radios crackle to life and we all check in on the assigned ground frequency—"One up, two up, three up, and four up." Since VMA-225 is closest to the south (takeoff end) of the field, we stay in our revetments until Lieutenant Colonel Stender and his wingman have taxied past us. Then I pull out, and Ron falls in behind me on the taxiway. We rock along the narrow aluminum taxiway and proceed to the JATO arming station. In succession we each arm the two rocket bottles for takeoff. Now we're ready to go flying!

We change channels to departure control and Lieutenant Colonel Stender leads the way. Taxiing into position, he goes to 80 percent power, checks his instruments, and then releases his brakes. Ten seconds later he ignites the JATO bottles and, in a giant cloud of smoke, disappears down the runway. By the time he has hit the JATO, number 2 aircraft is in position and as soon as number 1 was visible above the billowing rocket smoke, he starts his roll, and I follow him in sequence. As I clear the smoke haze, number 4, Ron Kleiboeker, goes through the same procedure.

In a matter of minutes, all four A4s are airborne. Following the lead, we all turn to the right out to sea and when clear of the land, pickle (release) the JATO bottles into the sea. Then Lieutenant Colonel Stender continues his climbing right turn and all three of us have joined him by the end of the first circle. As briefed, we join in a tactical four-plane division with his wingman on his right side and my section stacked on the left side.

The next chore is to locate the C130 tanker and top-off the fuel loads.

The tanker, as usual, is in a standard racetrack pattern at 20,000 feet and 280 knots. In the three months we have been in Vietnam, I have refueled on every mission, day and night. Whether flying alone or in a section, there has never been a problem. Although four-plane divisions are not common due to the preponderance of helicopter escort missions we are assigned, the task of finding the tanker remains the same.

The tanker is orbiting about fifty miles south of Chu Lai, along the route to our mission area. He is "on station," waiting for us.

As we continue our climb out, we pass through several layers of thick cirrus clouds. Above one layer is another. Between layers, visibility is restricted but not impossible.

We switch to the tanker frequency, as briefed. Voice contact is made and Colonel Stender heads in the direction of the tanker, or so we think. We are still a few thousand feet below the tanker's assigned altitude, again, as planned for safety reasons. The fifty-mile point comes and goes with no visual on the tanker. Keep in mind, the three wingmen are following the lead. We're concerned about our flying in relation to the lead, not looking for the tanker or where we may be over the ground. That's his problem to solve. That is, until it becomes our problem!

**C130 TANKER—FUELING DROGUES EXTENDED
TWO HARRIER JETS "PLUGGED IN"**

Apparently lost, Lieutenant Colonel Stender commences a right turn to find the tanker. Now no one knows where we are in relation to the C130. All relativity goes asunder. Then another turn, this time to the left. More of the same for twenty minutes. My oxygen mask is turning blue from the language I'm spewing into it. This really should not be a problem. But I'm not in a position to solve it.

Now I am anxiously watching our fuel state. Remember, we took off with ammo and little fuel. The choice is always one or the other but not both.

I'm also watching the DME (distance measuring equipment) that indicates our mileage from Chu Lai. Suddenly, for some unknown reason, Lieutenant Colonel Stender has chosen to head south and find the tanker sometime later. Instead of closing on the tanker, wherever it might be, we are now moving away from it!

I look at the instruments again; we are 120 miles south of Chu Lai. A mild state of panic starts to set in. I'm now quickly calculating how much fuel we have left to return to base. We certainly don't want to run short and have to punch-out in this neighborhood! It would be a very long walk home. I have been in this position before and don't want a repeat performance.

As we trundle south, I come to the realization that the A4Es are burning considerably less fuel than we are. The aircraft mismatch has become very obvious. Stender is paying absolutely no attention to his number 3 and number 4 wingmen. I have to make a decision immediately. I'll deal with the consequences later. We must get our two A4C aircraft on the ground quickly.

I key my microphone and announce to the lead, Lieutenant Colonel Stender:

"I am breaking off my section and returning to base."

It was neither a request nor a question. I look over at Ron, and he nods his approval. There is no return comment from the lead aircraft. He is lost in the moment.

With a nod of my head to the left, the two of us peel out of formation and head northeast toward the coastline and Chu Lai—120 long miles away. Suddenly the cockpit becomes even hotter, or at least it feels that way. Sweat is dripping from my helmet and down into my eyes and mask. My favorite smelly flight suit is totally drenched—again!

As we head north, I debate about trying to find the tanker. If we find each other, all is well. If I cannot find him, then we have committed ourselves to a bailout. There really is no decision to make. No tanker this trip, we are heading directly back to Chu Lai.

Leaving the tanker frequency, I contact Chu Lai Approach Control. I explain that we are unable to refuel and are heading home and would have low-fuel state by the time we arrive. They fully understand the situation as they have been monitoring the tanker frequency and listening to the refueling fiasco as it unfolded.

I calculate that it would take about twenty minutes to get both planes on the ground. One hundred-twenty miles divided by seven miles per minute equals seventeen minutes plus three to slow down and eventually land in sequence. Simple math, really. I had done this a hundred times before—although only a few times when flying on fumes.

Checking our fuel-burn rate, I conclude that even at 20,000 feet, with all the ordnance (bombs) we were carrying, we did not have sufficient fuel to get home. We are each lugging an even dozen five-hundred-pound bombs on the wings. The weight and the additional drag is causing us to burn fuel at a very high rate. Something has to go and go quickly!

We had angled toward the Vietnam coastline when starting back, just in case we had to jump out! I signal my wingman to follow me out over the water and descend to 10,000 feet. Powering back, we head down. Soon we're about a mile offshore and still heading north. I signal that we are going to jettison everything on the wings and "clean up" the airplane to give ourselves a chance to get back. He understands completely.

I place my left glove hand on the yellow and black "T" handle in the lower center of the instrument. It sits just in front of the stick and between my kneecaps. On the count of four, I yank the handle. I can feel the release on the stick. The plane seems to jump a couple of hundred feet. I look over at Ron and his bomb racks are on the way down as well.

We jettison the bomb racks and the bombs intact so they would not arm on the way down. Not that I really cared at that point—they are heading for "Davy Jones's Locker" in any event.

In the clean configuration, the A4 is a marvelous airplane. Now that we have dumped all the excess baggage, Chu Lai suddenly seems a lot closer. I set us up for a straight-in approach right up the coastline and in about ten minutes, we reduce power to idle and start down at 360 knots. The fuel gauges immediately reflect the loss of all the weight we left behind. We don't have any excess fuel, but at least we will get home. Suddenly the cockpit seems to get a bit cooler.

I signal Ron to move ahead and land first as I know he has less fuel than I do. It's always the case that a wingman burns more fuel than the lead due to the constant throttle movements required to maintain wing position. I fall a mile behind him and drop my hook, flaps, and gear. Just as he clears the runway I touch down, roll into the arresting wire, and stop. We have arrived home safely. My fuel gauge is hovering at the error limit of six hundred pounds. I assume that his is considerably less.

Now for the mission debrief.

Normally, the Marine Corps does not take lightly the jettisoning of perfectly good bomb racks – much less the ordnance hanging on them. However, in this case, the Group Commander and his Operation guys had been monitoring the flight from start to finish. The A4Es hadn't found either the tanker or the spotter and had finally aborted the mission. At the moment, they were struggling to get back to Chu Lai as well.

In fact, the two A4Es were only now approaching the base and have been ordered to drop the ordnance in the ocean before landing—not the bomb racks, only the bombs. Except for unexpended twenty-mm ammunition, we never, ever landed with live ordnance hanging on an aircraft.

Anticipating a reprimand at best, I am still steaming mad by the time we reach the debriefing tent. There is a muted silence everywhere. We are asked a few perfunctory questions. Then scoping out the scenery, we diplomatically express our feelings regarding the lunacy of mismatching two different type aircraft. I leave my professional feelings toward Lieutenant Colonel Stender still burned into my oxygen mask. With nothing further to be gained, we excuse ourselves and depart back to our tents. I never heard a further word about the bomb racks.

That was the first and last mission that combined A4Cs and A4Es.

RETURNING TO CHU LAI FROM THE NORTH

CHAPTER 14

Hong Kong, 1965
A Tragedy

I'VE BEEN AWAY FROM HOME for eleven months—eight since the emergency leave for my father and almost three months in Vietnam. Word filters down to the squadron that there are two rest and recreation (R&R) passes available to Hong Kong for four days. A lottery is quickly established. The usual tension is present, and Lieutenant Ron Kleiboeker and I are the lucky winners. The flight is a Marine Air Group 12 resupply run—not the daily C130 First Marine Air Wing shuttle flight to Hong Kong from Saigon via Da Nang.

Quickly digging a few moldy, wrinkled "civvies" out of my foot-locker, I join Ron on the muddy walk to the tarmac. Awaiting us is the group gooney bird. It is a WWII vintage Marine C47 that will take us to Hong Kong. I wouldn't be surprised if it had flown the "Hump" into Burma in the 1940s—it looks and smells of the jungle. However, it is our chariot for the weekend!

I am used to this very aircraft, having flown it in the previous winter up to Camp John Hay at Baguio in the Philippines. The seats are canvas and the air-conditioning consists of leaving a few of the windows open. The engine smells and sounds are different. The two prop engines on this plane are burning regular fuel, not the kerosene we use in jet engines. Although we can't hear each other over the engines, that does nothing to dampen our enthusiasm and relief of being out of the war zone, if only for a few days.

The flight is uneventful, and four hours later the mystical city of Hong Kong unfolds before us. Due to the position of Hong Kong Island, the approach into Kai-Tak Airport requires a clockwise circling descent past Hong Kong Island and over the apartments of Kowloon on the mainland. Without a doubt, it is the scariest approach to any major airport in the world. As we make the turning descent over the laundry lines and streets of Kowloon, I can see directly into the apartment windows. With the windows open, we can smell the cooking.

The single runway is oriented north-south and all takeoffs and landings are to the south, away from the city and out to the open sea. This feature will remain etched in my mind for the rest of my life, for reasons yet to be discovered.

Taxis are everywhere in Hong Kong. We jump in one and head for the President Hotel off Nathan Road on the Kowloon side. Checking in, we part for a welcome shower and quickly regroup for much-needed drinks. There is a cocktail bar in the basement that becomes our headquarters for the next three days. It is now Friday, and we are scheduled to depart late Tuesday morning.

In 1965, there are no tunnels between Kowloon and Hong Kong Island. The only access is by boat. For pedestrians it is the Star Ferry from multiple locations on both sides of the harbor. Our favorite port is the main ferry pier across from the Peninsula Hotel—a few blocks from the President Hotel. As luck would have it, there is also a terrific cocktail lounge and view of the harbor in the Peninsula.

Late Friday evening, I phone Judy in Iowa to inform her that I was safely out of Vietnam and not scheduled to return until Tuesday. The communications are by radio-telephone and suspect at best. Weather conditions determine the availability and quality of the connection— again, a factor in what lay ahead.

We visit all the obligatory sights: the Floating Market, Hong Kong peak, and the endless walks up and down the busy streets. Back and forth on the Star Ferry is the best way to really see Hong Kong and its magical skyline. The new Hilton Hotel had recently opened and is considered a "skyscraper" at twelve stories! It has since been replaced with the seventy-two-story Bank of China building, a real skyscraper. Today that all but disappears in the modern spectacular skyline.

The three days go by all too quickly.

It is now Tuesday morning, August 24, 1965, and Ron and I are standing at the check-out desk of the President Hotel. It is about 10:00 a.m. and we are to be at Kai Tek Airport for a noon takeoff. The airport is a short twenty-minute taxi ride away.

Abruptly the US Navy Shore Patrol and the Hong Kong Police approach us. Their identity is obvious. Without any chitchat, the police officer asks if we are Lieutenants Kane and Kleiboeker. Confirming our identity, we are then ordered to follow them. There has been an accident.

The regular R&R shuttle, a C130 Hercules, was scheduled for its 9:00 a.m. departure back to Vietnam. It had just gotten airborne with full power, heading south toward the South China Sea. Shortly after takeoff, one of the left (port) engines caught on fire and was shut down. There was still sufficient power to maintain flight on three engines. At 500 feet, the fire continued to burn so the pilot reached up to "feather" (neutralize) the propeller on the bad engine. The emergency feather knobs are on the overhead control panel between the pilot's and copilot's heads.

In reaching up, the pilot mashed the wrong button—he feathered the remaining good engine on the left side. Suddenly there was no power on the left side of the aircraft. This was compounded by the full thrust still churning on the right (starboard) side of the plane. The result was a disaster. The C130, with no power on the left side, plunged into the water that borders the runway.

Ironically, the pilot, copilot, and a few others on the flight deck survived. They managed to escape through the large side windows that surround the cockpit. It was the pilot's recount of the facts of the mishap that were reported accurately. There were seventy-one souls aboard the C130. Thirteen miraculously survived and fifty-eight other Marines were not so lucky. They perished in the crash.

The salvage operations are underway by the time Ron and I reach the city morgue in Kowloon. We are escorted into the building and back to the receiving dock. I had never been in a morgue. The illumination is stark fluorescent light bouncing off dirty white walls. The smells are the usual Asian ones mixed with an antiseptic overlay; a nauseating start to the gruesome task ahead.

Shortly after we arrive, the first bodies arrive. They are delivered by ambulance at first and then every other mode of emergency transportation available. Quickly the system becomes overwhelmed. The morgue "cold room" has a total of thirty drawers for corpses. Some are already occupied by John Does from the weekend's activities, leaving about twenty-five for our Marines. By the evening it becomes obvious that there are not enough boxes in the chiller to handle the number of casualties coming in.

Ron and I are the only Marines available in Hong Kong. The MAG12 C47 that we were on has been ordered back to Vietnam to fetch the investigation party. We aren't stranded—we are where we are supposed to be. There is no shortage of work to do.

As the Marines are delivered to the morgue, we immediately scour their wet pockets for identification. There is the usual Marine ID in waterproof plastic, as well as the dog tags. This is a very, very emotional task. Probing the sea-soaked uniforms for their ID photos and matching the faces is tough duty. Fortunately there has been no fire. I am not sure we could handle that!

Now the seawater smells attack the nostrils. With the loading-dock doors open, the air-cooling is gone and the temperature and humidity rise well into the nineties. My uniform is drenched in sweat. My shoes squish from the seawater flooding the dirty gray tile floor in the morgue.

The recovery operation continues through the night. By daybreak all the available cabinets have been filled. As the sun rises, the recoveries pick up. The plane's manifest indicates a total of fifty-eight Marines are dead or missing. We still have twenty-eight to go and no appropriate place to store them. Now the grotesque begins—we have no choice. The same routine for identification but then we have to physically stack the stiffening bodies one upon another in the chiller. This macabre sight still remains with me today.

All through today, Wednesday, it is more of the same. I think that sooner or later the door will cease opening and the temperature will cool down. But not today.

It is midday on Thursday when the last Marine has been recovered and delivered to the morgue. By this time, rigor mortis and bloating has set in, making identification much more difficult. Ron and I have been on duty for forty-eight hours. Other than an endless supply of Chinese tea, we have eaten nothing and have no appetite for food. I won't be able to eat solid food for a week.

With the steady supply of recovered Marines, it is impossible to leave the morgue. Ron and I identify and catalogue fifty-eight Marines in forty-eight hours. Accuracy is paramount in our minds. These are sons and husbands. Our fear is to send a false identification to the loved ones back home. The news is bad enough.

Finally, after almost fifty hours in the morgue, Ron and I are relieved. The investigation party has arrived from Vietnam. We are taken back to the President Hotel for a rest and a change of clothes. Food is not of any interest. Drinks are. We are too tired to sleep—plenty of time for that later.

My first priority is to get word back to Judy that I am okay. There is a typhoon somewhere in the Pacific and the radio-telephone linkage is spotty at best. My father's Wall Street contacts have been trying to get information on the crash. As days pass by and there is no word from me, they all assume that I have been killed in the crash.

Judy has told me very little over the years about the incident. Her parents had heard about the crash on the late TV news and headed into the town where she and the children lived while I was overseas. Assuming the worst, she did volunteer that there was a prayer service for me in her hometown, Blencoe, Iowa. I can only imagine what that was like for a mother of four toddlers.

On Friday morning, Thursday night at home, I finally manage to get a phone call through to my parents in New York. The relief is palpable. They immediately notify Judy of my safety.

Neither Judy nor my parents ever expanded on those days when I was presumed dead. They never volunteered any information and, frankly, although curious, I don't ask.

Late Friday afternoon, Ron and I jump aboard the C47 when it departs Hong Kong for Chu Lai.

It was twenty-two years before I returned to Hong Kong. It was on business in 1987. As we descended into Kai-Tek, my mind flashed back to 1965 and all the sad memories. Tears came to my eyes as we entered the familiar approach pattern over the tenements and land. As we slowed down on the runway, I looked east toward the water and docks where my fellow Marines perished. I have experienced some level of "survivor's remorse" all these years, thinking many, many times, *Why them and not me?*

Judy accompanied me on that trip back to Hong Kong but the incident was never discussed. This is the first time I have chosen to write of it.

A number of years after the Vietnam Memorial opened in Washington, the names of the fifty-eight Marines were inscribed on the Wall. A fitting tribute.

CHAPTER 15

Back To Pensacola

To BEGIN THIS STORY, I must set the stage. When preparing to leave Vietnam, I indicated my station preferences to the personnel department of the Marine Corps. Although I'm holding a "regular commission" as a captain in the Corps, which entitles me to stay aboard for a career, I have decided to separate when my five-year commitment is up.

Since deciding to accept the regular commission in 1961, my world has turned over. I am now married for almost four years and have a devoted wife and four young children. In addition, I am anxious to return to New York and pick up my fledgling career in Wall Street, a career that went on hold in 1961, when I came on active duty.

Sometimes, the Marine Corps operates in strange ways. I am literally one of the first pilots to return stateside since the buildup of forces in early 1965. I envision my talents will be best used in the Second Air Wing to help transition the newer pilots on their way to Vietnam. The Marine Corps, however, has another idea.

Now we begin the story.

Judy and I receive orders to report to the Air Station Command at Cherry Point. I am assigned the position of "Custodian" of the non-appropriated activities on the Air Station. Little do I realize I would never sit in the cockpit of an A4 Skyhawk again, or at least until forty years later when I fly one in Arizona.

In my new position, I'm responsible for the finances of all the recreational activities on the base and report directly to Major Cyrus Blanton, USMC, all five foot six of him.

The first day on base, I go through the routine paperwork at the Air Station headquarters and then set out for Major Blanton's office, which is located in the base gymnasium. I arrive in the uniform of the day and wait patiently to meet my new boss.

After a considerable delay, I am ushered into the Major's office and I present my papers. After a long scan, the good Major then proceeds to leave me at attention and tell me why he personally dislikes being assigned to an aviation facility and why, in particular, he detests aviators. For twenty minutes he rants about all that is wrong with his assignment and especially being stuck with me. He chants all of this in his best Georgia accent. I manage to control myself as I stare down at him. I don't know whether to laugh or punch him. I am then dismissed and told to go find a hole in which to crawl.

It is now late afternoon, and I depart for the base housing that Judy and I had been assigned the day before. I walk into the unit like a raving banshee. Amid all the four-letter words I was allowed in front of the kids, I relate the story and ask how the Marine gods could possibly do this to me? As usual, Judy is unflappable and finally calms me down.

The next day, I locate my appointed hole and settle into my new post fairly quickly, putting the previous year behind me. Events that had taken place in the Far East will stay with me for a long, long time, but I am unaware of it for the next twenty years. Unfortunately, Judy and the children bear the brunt of my behavior and problems for all that time, and more.

I finally admit that the new job as Custodian fits me well. My responsibilities, although financial, cover the gamut of social activities across the base. There are the Officer and Non-Commissioned Officer clubs, the Post Exchange and even the circus came to town in our gymnasium. It is all a bit of fun.

Eventually, I wear Major Blanton down. He is still miserable but no one can change that fact! His total disdain for pilots, especially me, melts away and he starts to pressure me to take him flying. Enlightened self-interest is a great motivator!

On the Air Station, there are pilots who need time in the air to remain qualified. And there are airplanes that need to be flown so they can remain operational. For me, it is a marriage made in heaven. Since most of the Air Station guys are multi-engine transport or helicopter drivers, I have my own private fleet of jets. There are two T2V jets needing airtime. Although dating back to the Korean War period, they are well maintained and, fortunately, fairly idiot-proof. And I am about to prove it!

The T2V is a Navy version of the famous Air Force F80 Shooting Star. I fondly remember the Strombecker wooden models that I made when still in school. It is straight-winged and has two large, three-hundred-gallon fuel tanks on the wing tips. Besides fuel, the tanks add a degree of stability that swept-wing aircraft later swapped for maneuverability.

To quiet the good Major down, I arrange for him to be checked out in the ejection seat and the pressure chamber. This, however, is not exciting enough for him—he actually wants to go flying!

LOCKHEED TV2 "SHOOTING STAR"

Despite its great looks and apparent ample fuel supply, the T2V has a very limited range. It can only go six hundred miles before refueling. That is far enough, however, as I have already determined to take Cyrus Blanton to the best Officer's Club in the Navy for Friday night Happy Hour. He is locked and loaded from the moment I mention it to him.

Mustin Beach Officers' Club in NAS Pensacola, Florida, was also the scene of our wedding three years earlier and many a celebration party since then.

It is a Friday in March, and we decide to launch from Cherry Point after lunch and arrive at Sherman Field, Pensacola, in time for Happy Hour. The Major has a commitment that dictates we be back at Cherry Point by noon on Saturday. That means I have to schedule an early Saturday morning departure from Pensacola.

The plane captain straps Major Blanton into the back seat, hooks up his oxygen mask, and radios that we are set to go. As usual with the T2V, the engine starting sequence is all manual and requires considerable skill in selecting which toggle switches to throw and in what sequence. Unlike the A4, nothing is automatic. Fortunately, with the help of the plane captain, a corporal, I manage to get the engine started. No problem here. He then arms the two ejection seats, I lower the large canopy, and we taxi out for takeoff.

With a full fuel load, the T2V takes a while to get airborne, and then it doesn't go very far. But it's fun to fly, and I actually enjoy having Major Blanton in the back seat. Since the Training Command, I have never flown an aircraft with a back seat. I point out the sights along the way, and he seems to weather the flight very well. The weather is clear and the journey uneventful. We land safely at Pensacola and check into the BOQ, shower, and head for the O Club.

The club is jumping. I can't believe that after fifteen years in the Marine Corps, Major Cyrus Blanton has never seen the likes of the "home" of Naval Aviation on a Friday night. As one of the very first pilots who have combat experience in Vietnam, I am in my glory. The rum and Cokes are going down like ice water. Cyrus, a southern boy, is into bourbon and something—anything. Then there are the "after-dinner" drinks. We jam some food into ourselves at some point in the evening but the damage has already been done.

We wrap up the celebration sometime before midnight and manage to get a ride back to the BOQ. We have adjoining rooms. I help the Major into his room and then collapse in my own bed. I have left a 0730 wakeup for a 0900 takeoff back to North Carolina.

Unfortunately, the wake-up call comes on time. I struggle out of the rack and jump into the shower, assuming that the Major is on the same track. A quick shave and I am dressed in my smelly flight suit and ready to go.

I grab my gear and head next door to meet the Major. The doors aren't locked—no need for that in the BOQ. I knock, get no answer, and knock again. Still no answer. I turn the knob and open the door. Sprawled across the bed, still in his happy-hour uniform, is Major Blanton. He is comatose. It is almost 0800, and we have a 0900 launch time. Thanks to him!

I manage to get the good Major up and into the shower. He comes around a bit but is still out of it. He struggles into his flight suit as I jam his party clothes into the B4 bag for the ride home. By now he is at least moving under his own steam as we head down to grab the shuttle to Sherman Field about a mile away.

We arrive at the flight line a few minutes late but not critical. I send Blanton to the aircraft with the ground crew and go into operations to file our flight plan. The weather is magnificent all the way to North Carolina on this quiet Saturday morning. The plan is straightforward—leave Pensacola, cross Alabama and southern Georgia, into South Carolina and then North Carolina, and down into Cherry Point. It will take us about two hours.

By the time I complete the flight plan and ride out to the airplane, Major Blanton has climbed aboard and the plane captain has strapped him in. He is ready to go. I have a preflight inspection to conduct. In the TV2 the speed brakes are situated under the aircraft extending down from the fuselage. The procedure, unlike the A4, was to leave the brakes extended so the hydraulic system could be checked for leaks prior to takeoff. I have complied as per the shut-down procedures and duly noted them down for inspection during my preflight. So much for that.

I climb up the ladder, a short one for the T2V, and slide into the ejection seat. I am really feeling hungover by now and the booze and sweat is starting to pour out in the humid morning air. Quickly hooking up my oxygen mask and plugging in my G-suit, the plane captain assists me in fastening my harness. Now, I am also ready to go.

I manage the complicated starting procedure successfully—very proudly for someone in my delicate condition. The engine roars to life. The dials jump to attention. I turn on the radio and ground control reads me our flight plan, as requested. I lower the large can-opy and check it down and locked. I give the thumbs-up for an okay and the chocks to be removed. Adding power, I swap salutes with the plane captain, and we are on our way home.

It is very quiet at Sherman Field at 0900 on a Saturday morn-ing. With no traffic, we are cleared to takeoff on the north runway toward Pensacola Bay and Pensacola City. The runway is eight thou-sand feet in length and dutifully marked every one thousand feet with distance-remaining signs. We bounce along the taxiway toward the Gulf of Mexico all the way to the end.

I wait for takeoff clearance from the tower before turning onto the runway. We are cleared for immediate takeoff and assigned a frequency on which to contact departure control after liftoff. "Have a good day" is our final message from the tower.

As the TV2 straightens out on the runway, I apply full power and we commence our takeoff roll. Everything seems natural. I glance over at the tower as we pass it. The four thousand foot marker slips past—power 100 percent rpm and speed 120 knots—still a little slow but nothing to worry about. The three thousand foot marker falls behind and we were still at 120 knots and on the runway. Suddenly I become concerned that the airplane should be starting to fly by now! We pass the two thousand foot marker! I double-check my power settings and airspeed—125 knots and still on the runway—not good news! Now I am really concerned. Sweat immediately starts to pour out of every pore in my body. As we pass the one thousand foot marker I'm staring at the blue water of Pensacola Bay in front of us—and getting closer!

One of the beauties of straight-wing aircraft is the ability to man-handle them without the plane biting back. Knowing we are at the speed that this aircraft should be flying, I gently but firmly rotate the nose up, however slightly. With about five hundred feet remaining on the runway, she struggles into the air. In that millisecond, I retract the landing gear to reduce drag. In a short distance they weren't going to be of use anyway. She starts to climb—very slowly at first and then just slowly. The end of the runway suddenly falls behind us and we are skimming across the bay and onto the city. By now, between the oxygen and total fear, I'm completely sober—not a hint of a hangover remains. Last night's rum and Cokes are all in my flight suit, my mask, and my shoes.

I check in with departure control as if all is normal although I am sure my voice is an octave higher than normal. Indicating no problem, I keep heading northeast toward Georgia. Before long we are fifty miles north of Pensacola and barely at 1,400 feet and 140 knots. Without thinking, I press the speed brake button on the throttle with my left thumb and the plane must jump a thousand feet. I have taken off with the speed brakes still deployed! I missed them in my preflight inspection! Normally, the tower visually checks all aircraft through binoculars when taxiing but either they were at the same party last night or, more probable, they lost sight of me when I taxied south and away from the tower.

Breathing a massive sigh of relief and a quick prayer of thanks, I pull the nose up and continue to climb to our assigned altitude of 27,000 feet. All is well that ends well, or so I thought!

Since start-up, taxiing, and takeoff, I was preoccupied with communications and the task of piloting a machine that had not yet been configured to fly. I haven't exchanged any words with the good Major. I was too busy trying to determine why the airplane was not performing as advertised.

In military aircraft, the microphones are enclosed in the oxygen masks. They have two positions: "hot" and "off." Hot means that the microphones are on internally all the time and, in addition to voice transmissions, normal breathing can be heard in the earpieces in the helmets. This is generally reassuring but somewhat annoying. The usual position is off unless the transmit button is depressed.

I level us at 27,000 feet and finally start to breathe normally. I have managed to dodge death once again. This was a serious screw-up that could have ruined our whole day. However, it is now behind us and sitting in my drenched flight suit, I can at least enjoy the scenery on the way home. No one needs to know the tale, unless Blanton shoots his mouth off. Come to think of it, how is the good Major getting along? I frankly forgot about him.

I call his name in my mouthpiece—nothing in return. I check and the microphone toggle is in the on position. I should be able to hear his breathing, if not his voice. Nothing! I look into the side-view mirrors—they're curved along the canopy bars and afford a limited view of the rear seat. It's impossible to see directly behind me due to the position of the ejection seat. I can barely make out the shape of the Major slumped down in his seat, leaning against the canopy. However, I still can't detect him breathing in my earpiece. I can hear myself but not him.

I immediately fear the worst—Blanton has asphyxiated himself and died. His mask must have come loose and in my flying quandary, I never took notice. He is my responsibility, and I screwed up. I now have a stiff in the back seat! What the hell am I going to do?

To make sure of my conviction, I slam the stick forward and bounce the Major off the canopy a few times. Then a few more times!

Nothing! He simply falls back down into a ball in the ejection seat. Not a whimper from him. He is definitely a goner, that's for sure.

What to do next? I grab the flight charts. We're coming up on an Air Force base in South Carolina. I could declare an emergency and land there. No, I don't like the idea of landing on an Air Force base with a corpse in the back seat. They will have an investigation and discover that he was stone drunk when we took off and I, the pilot in command, was not far behind him. My ass would be finished for sure. Enough of this emergency stuff!

We go a bit farther, and I think about altering the flight plan and landing at MCAS Beaufort, SC. At least on a Marine base I might have a fighting chance. It won't help Blanton, but in this business you have to expect losses! This is my alcohol-induced thought process!

Just as I am about to trigger the microphone and alter the flight-plan to MCAS Beaufort, I hear this god-awful sound in my earpiece. It is Blanton finally surfacing. He has risen from the dead—or at least that's what is going through my mind. At first there is a great sense of relief. Then a feeling of outrage catches up with me. This stupid bastard has managed to ruin my flight back to Cherry Point, and I missed all the sights along the way.

I contain my anger and am very grateful that I hadn't yet declared an emergency. That would have been very difficult to explain to anyone, especially Major Blanton.

We continue the flight home and start our letdown as we cross the North Carolina border. All the excitement is now behind me, thank God! A routine approach, speed brakes down (it seems they had hardly been up), flaps down, and finally gear down. Steady at 120 knots and a gentle touchdown—this airplane is not designed or stressed for the usual "carrier" landing. And this morning, neither am I!

After we taxi in and deplane, I asked the Major how he enjoyed the flight. I get the usual razzle-dazzle but he knows that I know better. He is embarrassed, and I like it that way. From that date forward until my separation, Major Cyrus Blanton is no longer a problem for me.

Thank God he was also oblivious to our takeoff fiasco, and I didn't tell him anything! It would have scared the hell out of him and evened the score.

A few years later, he was retired from the Corps for personal transgressions. It seemed to me a fitting end for a Marine who didn't like aviators!

CHAPTER 16

Forty Years Later

JUDY AND I HAD PUT my flying days well behind us. In 2001, we were embedded in the development of Adare Manor, our hotel in Ireland. Beginning in 1999, when we hosted the display of the traveling Vietnam Wall Memorial on the grounds of Adare Manor, we decided to fly the Marine Corps flag amid the Irish and American flags in front of the golf clubhouse.

It was a typical overcast day when a gentleman named Jim Moriarty stopped by for lunch and inquired about the Marine Corps flag. Needless to say, Jim was a Marine. I happened to be in the clubhouse and introduced myself, and we struck up a conversation that has lasted for years.

Jim is currently serving with me on the Board of the Marine Corps Museum in Quantico.

Jim had engineered a purchase from the Israeli government of ten A4N and TA4 Skyhawk jet fighters for use in a private squadron in Arizona that flew government-contract training flights. To no surprise, it was less expensive to station an A4 for a training sortie than either an F16 or F18.

Jim waited at Adare Manor for several days as the two ferry pilots cleared the airplanes out of Israel and traversed the Mediterranean from Malta to Nice and thence onward to Shannon Airport, from which they would launch out across the North Atlantic.

After arriving in Ireland, I had the opportunity to meet the pilots and immediately struck up a now long-standing friendship with one of them, Ron Reagan, affectionately known as "the Guv." The time spent with Ron in Adare was a throwback to my old squadron days. Ron was a naval aviator about ten years behind me and also flew for the Marine Corps. After separating from active duty and joining American Airlines, he also joined the only flying reserve unit available and transferred to the Air Force.

Ron had just retired from both American (as a 777 pilot) and the Air Force (as a colonel) and was freelance flying every manner of aircraft around the world. In this case, he and a buddy were transporting two TA4s (two-seat version) from Israel to Arizona. He was stocking his own lair—these were among the fleet that would eventually number ten aircraft that he would ultimately fly for ATAC on commercial contracts.

After a few days of rest and golf, and certifying the weather to Keflavik, they decided to launch.

Jim and I had greeted them upon arrival so I had seen the aircraft. My envy was showing!

Ron filed his flight plan and fastened a GPS indicator to the windshield for navigation—he had purchased them in Limerick the day before! Jim was going to ride the back seat home.

Ron is a very fit but stocky guy, so helping strap him into the A4 cockpit was interesting. If I had a shoehorn, it would have helped. Little did I know I was calling the kettle black. Jim is rather slender, so he posed no similar problem.

In any event, they had the APU roaring away, and the air was hooked into the engine for starting. The familiar smells of the jet fuel and the whine of the APU brought back so many memories. If they had another set of flight gear, I would have talked my way onto the second plane.

When they were set, Ron gave the thumbs-up and the air flowed into the compressor. The roar changed to a high-pitched whine as the jet engine started to spin. He hit the igniters, and the low rumble of the engine took over and started its melodic climb when the thump of ignition was heard. I was in heaven. The sounds, the smells—all of it was so familiar some forty years ago!

They taxied out to the Shannon runway and lifted off to the west and then turned right heading past the Cliffs of Moher and out over the Atlantic, six hundred miles until landfall in Iceland, assuming the GPS locators were accurate.

They made the journey to Keflavik, Gander, Portland, Cleveland, and Denver, where Jim departed. Ron and his wingman flew on to Williams-Gateway Airport in Phoenix.

A few years pass but I had stayed in touch with Jim and Ron, who had joined the Adare Golf Club. Then I get a phone call from the third partner in the triumvirate, Jon McBride, who is a retired Navy captain, fellow Vietnam combat pilot, and an astronaut. At that time he was president of ATSI. He asks me if I want to go for a ride in one of their A4s—a silly question for sure. I make arrangements and set out for Phoenix the next week.

I want to get there before they change their minds!

Jon and Ron meet me at the airport, and after a few drinks, we have dinner. I'm starting to get torqued up not knowing what lay in store for me the next day. Jon has a crash pad to live in, and I stay with him that evening. He had been an F4 driver in the Navy before entering the astronaut program, so we had a great visit swapping sea stories. Jon had sixty-four missions in Vietnam, and I only had my sixty-three missions working for me!

The morning is typical for Arizona—semi-hot but not unbearable. Jon and I set out for the airport. Quietly, my anxiety starts to build. It has been forty years since I had last flown a tactical jet. Riding a bicycle? We shall see, I thought.

When we get to the airport, Ron takes over. To Ron, flying is his business and he has his flying hat on for sure. My anxiety starts to ease up.

It was like flight school. He sits me in the simulator, briefs me on the starting sequence, which I thought strange, and then outfits me in a flight suit, torso harness, G-suit, helmet, and mask. If I thought Ron was snug in Ireland, I feel like Houdini getting into all the gear.

Without further delay, Ron and I head to the flight line. Ten planes are lined up in a row, and we proceed to our aircraft. As we approach the plane, I assume that I will ride in the back. My mistake!

2006—TOM KANE WITH RON "THE GUV" REAGAN

Without hesitation, Ron says, "You get up front and I'll ride in the back and take pictures." I think he's kidding me until he guides me to the front ladder and orders me up. The plane captain is there and he assists me into the cockpit and proceeds to strap me in—the harness to the ejection seat, the G-suit to the eyeball socket, the oxygen to the mask, the radio cable from my mask and helmet to the proper cords. In about five minutes I'm absolutely soaked—a familiar feeling—but I'm ready to go flying!

The mics are hot and Ron checks in with me—I believe to see if I'm up for the match. I am and by now all my anxiety has totally disappeared. I'm in familiar territory now, although a bit cramped! The rush of pure oxygen settles me down as it had so many times in the past, although by now I haven't touched liquor in six years. It's almost a waste of good oxygen.

The APU roars to life next to me on the right side—the ever-present aroma of jet fuel and tight fit in the cockpit. The plane captain is at two o'clock just below me. He stares at me for a signal. Instinctively I put my index finger in the air and rotate it to begin the ignition sequence. Immediately he throws the toggle on the APU and the compressed air whooshes into the engine compressors. I watched the rpm indicator and when it hits 5 percent, I push the throttle around the detent and wait. Four or five seconds go by, the rpm indicates 16 percent, and then the familiar dull, throaty rumble of ignition takes over the engine. When the rpms hit 45 percent, I instinctively give him the "plugs out" (thumb out from the flat palm) signal and he cuts off the APU. The screeching goes away and the ever-higher pitch of the engine takes over. The plane is under its own power now. The rpm indicator stops climbing at 60 percent idle while the EGT rises almost to its limit before the increased rpms bring it back down to normal.

I reach back on my right side and push in all the circuit breakers I can feel. The main gyro cages itself in an ever-dampening dance. The navigation needles rotate wildly until they lock onto their beacons. The radio comes to life, and I hear Ron calling my name and telling me that, so far, all is well. With almost one thousand hours in the A4, at least I can still start it. Needless to say, I am still in the chocks!

Ron handles the radio transmissions for the entire flight—I call it enlightened self-interest. For me it would have been like texting and driving at the same time. No safe way to do it—keep my eyes on the radio or in the air—but not both!

All checks complete, Ron calls for taxi instructions. We are directed to the duty runway and cleared out of the chocks and onto the taxiway. The airplane has "nose-wheel steering" activated by depressing a button on the stick. The only nose-wheel steering aircraft I have flown on a steady basis was the Grumman F11 at Beeville, Texas, forty-three years earlier. The A4s that I flew were single-seat versions and steered by differential pressure on the rudder pedals on the floor. Depressing the top of the rudder pedals activates the brakes individually to provide differential steering on the ground.

We start down the seemingly endless taxiway toward the runway. I know it is the active runway because I can see other planes landing and taking off in the distance. I keep the button depressed to steer the aircraft down the taxiway. However, even at idle rpm, the aircraft starts to gain speed, and I feel a need to slow it down.

Here's where the fun begins.

I need to elevate my legs to place my toes on the top of the rudder pedals and slow down the speed. As I try to raise first my right and then my left leg, my shins are hitting the bottom of the control panel, restricting my movement. I reach the seat toggle switch to lower the ejection seat all the way down—no problem. However, the plane continues to accelerate while I fiddle around.

I also realize that I will need to use my hands to lift each leg to get it high enough to reach the top of each brake pedal! To do that I have to release the steering button and let the plane drift. I do my right foot first, onto the pedal and right brake. As I enjoy my limited success, when I depress the right brake, the plane logically veers to the right. I quickly get my finger back on the steering button to correct the plane back to the centerline. Then, once again releasing the button, I grab my left leg and repeat the same gymnastic maneuver on the left pedal. The plane starts veering to the left. However, I am safely bunched up in the cockpit with both of my legs jammed against my chest.

Ron, sitting in the back seat, with a full set of controls that he never touched, yells into his mask/hot-mic:

"What the hell are you doing? We're all over the taxiway."

My only answer is the truth:

"Hey boss, I have forty pounds more between my asshole and my belly button than I had the last time I flew this plane. Cut me some slack!"

Ron's laughter roars in my ear, and I'm desperate to hold my feet up on the pedals, lest they get away again!

We arrive at the runway finally and are cleared into position for takeoff. As I turn onto the runway, I let my heels hit the floor and steadily add power. The A4 surges forward, and with that movement, all my residual apprehension evaporates. I am back home forty years later.

The takeoff roll goes quickly and soon I rotate the nose and ease into the air. Instinctively I retract the gear and flaps and feed in a little nose-down trim as we accelerate to 240 knots by the end of the runway. We are cleared for a right turn after takeoff and climb as we continue to gain speed. I settle down to a 360-knot climb on our way to 15,000 feet—just below the controlled airspace above 18,000 feet. I take a brief moment to look around at the surrounding desert—still mostly a featureless beige as I remember our days at Yuma in 1963. I think to myself, same church, different pew.

As we reach 15,000 feet and enter the Air Force–controlled practice space at 420 knots, Ron asks how I am doing. Meanwhile, he is taking photos.

He says:

"Are you ready to go to work?"

I answer in the affirmative, and he orders:

"Give me a four-g, three-hundred-sixty-degree turn to the right—now!"

Surprised, but without hesitation, I bank the plane to the right and yank the stick back until the g-meter reads 4.0. The mask is against my chest, and I am looking out the top of my eyeballs at the two instruments that matter—the g-meter and the altimeter. I surprise myself in the ability to hold the altitude very well while turning like a corkscrew. Three hundred sixty degrees later, I roll the wings level and reduce the stick pressure to neutral. The sweat starts to fill my mask and flight suit. It is obviously game on! This is the most physical work I have done in years!

Before I can settle down and admire my handiwork, Ron barks the next instruction:

"Give me a barrel roll—now."

I pull the nose up about fifteen degrees above the horizon and move the stick sharply to the right and keep it there. I think, don't snap it, roll it. I go around the three-hundred sixty-degree clock and stop rolling when the horizon approaches level. I always enjoyed barrel rolls, although I never felt comfortable stopping midway and flying upside down for more than a few seconds.

How the Blue Angels do it always amazes me.

Again the sweat continues to pour out of every pore in my body.

"How about a loop—now."

I push up the power to max rpm and drop the nose to accelerate from 420 to 480 knots. At 480 knots I commence a steady four-g pull-up by burying the stick in my stomach and concentrating on the g-meter and the gyro compass. Again, the G-suit fully inflates, pushing the air out of my lungs. As the nose climbs to the heavens, the attitude gyro rotates toward me, and I ride the longitude line up and through the vertical with the plane slowing, over the top. As we float upside down past the top, I have a chance to align my wings with the horizon, albeit upside down. I am off about ten degrees—not bad!

The nose comes down through the horizon and the airspeed picks up. In a few seconds, we pass the vertical and point straight down. The plane accelerates itself with the gravity at work, so I slowly pull back on the throttle to steady the speed back to 420 knots. The plane and the two of us are as one at the time—what a familiar thrill.

Ron follows with an "Immelmann"—a loop that rolls out on top to level flight. I haven't done one since flight school but off we go. No problem.

Then we do something I frankly have never done before in an A4: a deliberate stall. The maneuver is usually avoided due to heavy ordnance on the wings, but no other sane reason not to do it.

I pull the nose up to a sixty-degree climb angle and reduce the power to idle. As you can imagine, we very quickly run out of airspeed. I watch the airspeed indicator as it unwinds to zero, indicating there is no air flowing over the wings. We are no longer flying in the true sense of the word. We are literally falling out of the sky backward!

However, the engine turbine is still turning clockwise at 60 percent rpm, even at idle. Although not sufficient power to propel the airplane, the torque created by the clockwise motion of the rotator section of the compressor creates an opposite force that rotates the aircraft to the left. Ever so slowly the nose starts to fall to the left with no guidance from me. When it falls beneath the horizon and we head downhill, we start to gain speed, slowly at first and then very quickly. Soon we accelerate to normal flying speed and the controls are again usable. When we reach 250 knots, I add power and level off, accelerating to 420 knots—our normal speed.

I had experienced this law of physics before in the T34, a prop aircraft with the propeller turning to the right and the engine creating the same dynamic to the left, then we kicked rudder and deliberately induced a spin from which to recover. I am not about to spin the A4 at this point in my life.

After the aerobatics, we cruise around the area and do a bit of sightseeing. Again Ron has the camera at work behind me. We can still see the Williams-Gateway Airport in the distance and Ron tells me to head for it.

When we get to twenty-five miles from the airport, I slow to 250 knots and head toward the duty runway in a slow descent. Ron radios the tower and requests some practice landings. We are cleared to enter the pattern, and I cross the runway numbers at one thousand feet and 250 knots. They are using a right-hand landing pattern so at midfield I break right at forty-five degrees—too skittish to break at sixty degrees— and chop power to idle and pop the speed brakes. When we slow to 180 knots, I drop the gear and the flaps for landing. Now my challenge is to get the aircraft on the ground in condition for us to be able to walk away!

"ON TURNING FINAL—RUNWAY IN SIGHT"

I must confess that my landing pattern is not as tight as a shipboard approach—by a lot. Ron's photos attest to that fact. However, I make five good landings and four takeoffs while in the pattern. On the fifth landing, I pull off the power and we roll to a taxi speed. For some reason, I find it easier to navigate the brakes and the nose-wheel steering on the way back to the flight line. The taxi ride seems to go a lot quicker and before we know it, I am following the guy with the wands into our parking space.

TOM AND RON—INTO THE CHOCKS FOR THE LAST TIME

I had defied death once again, thanks to Ron Reagan who never touched the controls.

My only mistake was an early shutdown during the post-flight inspection, and it cost me a case of beer! It was worth many more cases.

When the chocks are in, and the plane shutdown, my flying career has officially come to an end! Forty years and forty pounds later (1966–2006), I can live with that realization.

Little did I ever conceive that my forty-year dream would come true. As the old ditty goes, it's a long way to Tipperary. This time I went from Adare to Phoenix.

My eternal thanks to Jim Moriarty, Jon McBride, and Ron Reagan for helping me live my dream.

THE END

JON MCBRIDE—A NAVY F4 PHANTOM DRIVER, SIXTY-FOUR COMBAT MISSIONS, AND SHUTTLE PILOT—MY SPONSOR AND FRIEND

TOM DAHONEY—VMA-225 MATE
DOWN FROM FLAGSTAFF TO SHARE MY LAST FLIGHT

FORTY YEARS LATER

THE KANE/COSGROVE FAMILY

**GERARD, DIANE, JUDY, TOM, LINDA, DARIA, TOM JR.,
TERI, GRACE, CONOR, FRANK, JOHN, ALENA,
LISANNE**

Epilogue

NOW THAT WE HAVE COMPLETED the journey, I hope you have enjoyed the ride. If, even for a second, you felt the sensations of sitting in the cockpit of a fast-moving jet, I have succeeded in my mission.

Need I point out that the 1960s were cavalier days for Marine aviation, and perhaps my anecdotes convey a sense of looseness in the ranks? That is certainly not my intention. The hours of ground study followed by endless training flights reflected a serious approach to the risky business at hand. Otherwise I could not have committed the errors outlined and managed to walk away unscathed.

In addition, the times were indeed different. My squadron, VMA-225, like many others, was a "band of brothers" with big, fast toys at our disposal. Working hard and playing hard was a way of life. Officers' clubs were the centers of the social scene on all bases—home and away. Drinking, often to excess, was part of the culture at the time. Unfortunately, like many others, I continued to feed the disease for decades after leaving the Corps. Perhaps it was my way of dealing with the tragedies of chapters 6 and 14— we'll never know.

In today's Marine Corps, a number of the episodes in this book would have cost me my career. I'm not saying today is better or worse—just different!

I feel blessed for the time spent in and around Marine Corps aviation. In a sense, the Corps gave me Judy and the children and all that followed from there, and for that, we shall be ever grateful.

Semper Fi,

Tom Kane

FOOTNOTE:

All profits from this book are dedicated to OPERATION SMILE and all the volunteers worldwide who change lives, one smile at a time. The Kane Family has been associated with the Magee Family, the founders, for almost thirty years, and I have enjoyed the honor of being Chairman Emeritus for many of those years.

Printed in Great Britain
by Amazon